DEFENSELESS FLOWER

A New Reading of the Bible

Carlos Mesters

Translated from the Portuguese by
Francis McDonagh

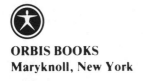

ORBIS BOOKS
Maryknoll, New York

**CATHOLIC INSTITUTE FOR
INTERNATIONAL RELATIONS**
London, England

Second Printing, March 1991

The Catholic Foreign Mission Society of America (Maryknoll) recruits and trains people for overseas missionary service. Through Orbis Books, Maryknoll aims to foster the international dialogue that is essential to mission. The books published, however, reflect the opinions of their authors and are not meant to represent the official position of the society.

Originally published as *Flor Sem Defesa: Uma Explicação da Bíblia a Partir do Povo* © 1983 by Editora Vozes Ltda., Petrópolis, Brazil

English translation © 1989 by Orbis Books

Published in the United States of America by Orbis Books, Maryknoll, NY 10545
Published in Great Britain by Catholic Institute for International Relations, 22 Coleman Fields, London NI 7AF

Manufactured in the United States of America

Library of Congress Cataloging-in-Publication-Data

Mesters, Carlos.
   [Flor sem defesa. English]
   Defenseless flower : a new reading of the Bible / Carlos Mesters : translated from the Portuguese by Francis McDonagh.
     p. cm.
   Translation of: Flor sem defesa.
   ISBN 0-88344-596-4
   1. Bible—Criticism, interpretation, etc.—Latin America.
2. Bible—Use. 3. Latin America—Religious life and customs.
I. Title.
BS517.2.M46   1989
220.6'098—dc20   89-35761
                                            CIP

ORBIS/ISBN 0-88344-596-4
CIIR/ISBN 1 85287 055 9

Contents

Foreword to the English Edition

This book came into being through the initiative of a friend of mine at Vozes, the Brazilian publisher. He put together these articles, which he felt were influential and spoke to the current situation in the church. The articles are meant to be like photographs that capture the life, joy, and suffering of people engaged in a richly complex action that bears great promise and hope for all. In the case of this book, the photographs are of the poor of Latin America interpreting the Bible in their communities. Some of the photographs and the persons they depict may have aged slightly, but the process they portray is as vibrant today as it was when I wrote the articles, and the process of the poor interpreting the Bible has, if anything, grown in importance in the last few years.

The contents of the book are varied. Chapter 1 is an article that was written in 1980 for the journal *Concilium*; it was part of an issue devoted to hermeneutics. Chapter 2, "The Light Breeze," is a reflection on the way the Bible was used and interpreted by the people of the base communities when they came together at the Third Inter-Ecclesial Meeting of the Basic Communities, held in João Pessoa, Brazil, in 1979. Chapter 3, "Defenseless Flower," is a reflection, with very different emphases, on the Second Inter-Ecclesial Meeting of the Basic Communities, held in Vitória in 1977. Chapter 4, "Biblical Theology in Brazil Today," was written for discussion at an informal meeting between theologians and the bishops on the Doctrine and Faith Commission of the Brazilian Bishops' Conference. It is not an official text. The epilogue of the book is made up of two prayers which speak for themselves and are undated, like, for example, most of the Psalms in the Bible.

Though the articles are varied, they all reflect one journey.

The book is intended to convey something of the important new phenomenon which the Spirit of God is calling into being in Latin America. It describes what has happened and what continues to happen among the poor when they use and interpret the Bible in the midst of their day-to-day lives. It seeks to convey something of the good news which runs through the life of the poor and their interpretation of the Bible and which they proclaim to the four winds. This good news—nourished by the blood, suffering, and joy of the poor—is, at least in part, the "defenseless flower" blooming in the hinterlands, backwaters, and slums of Latin America. If some part, however small, of this good news reaches the readers of the English translation of my book, I shall be very pleased.

The last sentence of the epigraph to chapter 3 says: "The world is growing afraid of you, defenseless flower!" When I wrote that sentence in 1973 I was thinking of the fear the flower produced in the generals and the capitalists. And they were afraid, as they still are. That is why they persecute and kill. Today, however, that sentence is beginning to reflect the situation in the church also. A few years ago there was the attack on the theology of liberation. The theology of liberation is the product of the use the poor make of the Bible in their communities. That use of the Bible is the source of their freedom in the face of the abuses of power. The last line of the epigraph continues to be true: "The world is growing afraid of you, defenseless flower!"

Belo Horizonte, Brazil
February 15, 1989

1

The Interpretation of the Bible in Basic Ecclesial Communities

Directly after this he made his disciples get into the boat and go on ahead to Bethsaida, while he himself sent the crowd away. After saying good-bye to them he went off into the hills to pray. When evening came, the boat was far out on the lake, and he was alone on the land. He could see they were worn out with rowing, for the wind was against them; and about the fourth watch of the night he came toward them, walking on the lake. He was going to pass them by, but when they saw him walking on the lake they thought it was a ghost and cried out; for they had all seen him and were terrified. But he at once spoke to them, and said, "Courage! It is I! Do not be afraid." Then he got into the boat with them, and the wind dropped. They were utterly and completely dumbfounded, because they had not seen what the miracle of the loaves meant; their minds were closed.

The challenges raised by biblical interpretation vary from continent to continent and depend largely on the culture of the people who read the text. Take a text like Mark 6:45–52, which describes the incident of Jesus walking on water. Standard European interpretation is determined by the fact that the exegete is talking to secularized people who have serious objections to such texts and cannot accept that someone can walk on water or calm the wind. In contrast, in Latin America the exegete is talking, not to a secularized or *nonbelieving* people, but to a profoundly religious and believing people who live in nonhuman conditions. They are a people exploited in many cases with the tacit support of the church itself. In Latin America the crisis of faith is not caused primarily by secularization, but by diabolical forms of oppression, which are often promoted by nations and peoples which call themselves Christian.

The difficulties raised by the Markan text vary not only from continent to continent, but also within the individual countries of Latin America. Within Brazil, for instance, interpretations vary depending on the persons reading the text: whether they are upper-class, whether they are poor but nonparticipants in the life of the basic communities, whether they are pastoral workers with some experience of reflecting critically on the social situation, or whether they are participants in the basic communities.

The great majority of people in the basic ecclesial communities are poor or, more exactly, impoverished by the oppressive capitalist system; they are farmers, workers, people from the outskirts of the big cities, farmhands, day-laborers, occasional workers, migrants, domestic servants, laundry-women, squatters, and so forth. When these people deal with the Bible their attitude is not (yet) secularized. For them the Bible is the word of God giving them God's message *today*. This faith determines how they see the text and conditions their whole interpretation.

They accept texts like the one from Mark naturally. Their approach to interpretation is very like that of the Church Fathers: they do not stop at the text-in-itself or the facts related by the text, but these become a base and a starting-point for discovering a deeper meaning which has to do with their own lives and the situation in which they live.

When they discuss a text the people at the same time discuss their own situation, without making much of a distinction, either on the level of methodology or content. Biblical history, without ceasing to be history, becomes a symbol or a mirror of the present situation as the people experience it in their community. Life and Bible mix. There is both mutual interference and illumination.

SOME EXAMPLES

Here are some examples which show a number of settings within which the people of the Brazilian basic communities read and interpret biblical texts. The examples also illustrate something about the effects of those settings upon the people's interpretation of specific texts.

1. In a Bible study group made up of farmers there was a discussion of Acts 12:1–17; the discussion focused on who the angel might have been who freed Peter from prison. Two interpretations were put forward. The first came from Senhor José, who said:

I was ill, but I said to myself, "This illness will not stop me from taking part in the Bible group" For me the illness was a prison which confined me to my bed. But there was another side to it: The illness helped me to see how much people cared for me—I never saw so many people in my house. There were lots of people in St. Peter's house too. Even Padre Henrique came to visit me. He came in and talked to me. When he left I started to get better; I got up and went to the meeting. If it had been in biblical times, people would have said that it was an angel of God who had freed me from my illness. And in a way it was!

The second explanation came from Dona Maria. She said:

When Dom Pedro Casaldáliga [the bishop of São Félix do Araguaia, Brazil, and a supporter of the communities] was a prisoner in his house, no one knew. There was no means of communication. Seven well-armed police officers kept watch at the house and refused to let anyone enter or leave. Exactly like Peter's prison in the Bible. But a young girl went in. No one took any notice of her. She was an ordinary girl, in cheap flip-flops. She took a note from Dom Pedro out of his prison, went straight to the airstrip, got a lift to Goiânia, and told the bishops who were meeting there. They got busy and got Dom Pedro freed. The girl was the angel of God who made the gates of Peter's prison swing open!

2. In one of the slums on the outskirts of Recife, a woman, a member of one of the basic communities, was arrested and thrown into a police car. She was very frightened and began to pray, "Jesus, I'm afraid. I'm so frightened I'm capable of betraying my friends. But the gospel tells us not to be afraid when we're taken before courts. And it tells us not to worry about what words to use to the police chief. Well, help me to conquer this fear and speak for me." But her fear increased. When she reached the police station her legs were shaking. She went in, terrified. But when the doors of the sergeant's office opened, as she put it, "Strength came up through my legs, the fear vanished, and such wonderful words came out of my mouth that I was amazed at myself. I thanked Jesus because I found that what the gospel says is really true!"

3. In a small basic ecclesial community made up of very poor farmers, the group read the text which prohibits the eating of pork. The people present at the meeting asked, "What message does God have to give us today through this text?" They discussed the matter and decided, "Through this text God wants to tell us that we, today, should eat pork!" The argument went as follows:

> God's main concern is with the health and life of God's people. Pork, when it's not treated properly, can cause disease and lead to death. Therefore in biblical times God forbade the people to eat pork. But today we know how to treat this type of meat. It's no longer a danger to our health. Besides that, it's the only meat we have to eat. If we don't eat this meat we'll be endangering the lives and health of our children. So today we ought to eat pork. That's being faithful to God!

4. In a gathering of different communities, a woman worker from São Paulo gave a commentary on the first reading of the Mass, which referred to the cry of the people (see Ex. 2:23–25). She said:

The Bible says that God heard the people's *cry*. It doesn't say God heard the people's *prayer*. I don't mean we shouldn't pray. I mean we should imitate God. Many people work first to get the people to pray and join the community. Only after that do they hear their cry. But I think our work ought to be directed, first of all, at all the people who suffer and weep, and their cry ought to get through to us!

5. In a slum of Recife a woman said to a Sister, "Sister, God came to my house today!" The Sister replied, "What do you mean?" The woman said, "I didn't have the money to pay for medicine for my son, who's sick. My neighbor earned money doing laundry for a whole week. It was one hundred cruzeiros, and she gave it all to me to buy the medicine. That could only be God, don't you think?"

These interpretations, so simple and so true, both as regards the Bible and as regards life, show something of the attitude to interpretation among the people of the communities. There are three important elements in this attitude to interpretation which need to be analyzed in more detail. They can be summed up under the following headings: freedom, familiarity, and fidelity.

FEATURES OF POPULAR EXEGESIS

Freedom with the Biblical Text

The people of the communities are able to treat the Bible with great freedom. This freedom is not the fruit of an argument developed by a better educated pastoral worker; nor is it the result of a careful literary study the people have learned from some exegete (nor could it be, since many of the people are illiterate; they do not understand exegetes' reasoning, which comes from another culture). In the examples I have described this freedom appears as the almost natural fruit of communal, lived experience. Other religious groups of the poor—groups which shut out this communal, liberating experience of faith—

tend to get imprisoned in the letter of the text and fall into a narrow fundamentalism.

The Bible on its own is not enough to produce this freedom. On its own the Bible can only set the heart on fire (see Lk. 24:32). For the Bible to release its meaning, there has to be a new experience of life, an experience of resurrection (see Lk. 24:28–30). Only in this way do eyes open (see Lk. 24:31) and the people begin to see the meaning of the Bible for their lives.

This liberation from the prison of the letter through lived experience is the first step in a long process. Sometimes even the pastoral workers do not realize the importance of this first step. More rational in their concerns, they try to free the people from the prison of the letter by means of questions about historicity: "Did that really happen? Did the angel really go into Peter's prison? Did Jesus really walk on water?" These questions are important, but they are not the most important questions to set off the process of interpretation.

What is much more important is to pay attention to two things which generate in the people this freedom with the biblical text: (1) the value of the symbolic element in life and events; (2) the overall process taking place in the particular church to which the communities belong.

On the point of symbolism, questions about historicity do not come first in the concerns of the people of the communities. The examples described above show that they are neither fundamentalist nor historicist. Even though they accept a text without question, this does not mean that they take it literally. The interpretation of the angel appearing in Peter's prison is proof of this. We who belong to a more rational culture have discovered the value of the symbolic after a long process of demythologization. For the people symbols are a real dimension of their lives. By an unconscious intuition they see the symbolic value of the facts narrated by the texts because they interpret the events of their own lives in exactly the same way. And this is the place to say that a symbolic explanation of the facts is not always the product of a naive, uncritical, or prescientific understanding. The people themselves are already beginning to understand that not everything can be explained in a symbolic way. In a meeting of ninety farmers, many of them illiterate, the farmers themselves raised the question: "How do we know when a text should be explained literally and when not?" After breaking up into groups, in which they discussed the question, they gave the following answer: "The text is not to be taken literally (1) when it doesn't fit our situation, and (2) when Jesus tells us to change for the sake of the commandment to love."

The other factor which enables the people to be so free with the biblical text is the overall process of the local church to which the communities belong. This brings us to the second point.

Familiarity

These examples of popular interpretation reveal a familiarity in dealing with the biblical text. It is not the familiarity of people who know the Bible from beginning to end, but that of people who feel at home in the Bible. Before the movement of renewal through the basic communities began, the Bible was always on the side of those who teach, give orders, and hand out pay, and it was explained in a way that confirmed the knowledge of those who taught, the power of those who gave orders, and the wealth of those who paid. Now the Bible is beginning to be on the side of those who are taught, ordered, and paid, and these people are discovering exactly the opposite of what was always considered the teaching confirmed by the Bible.

Gradually the Bible is ceasing to be for them a strange book which belongs to the "others," to the "Father," the "doctor," the "boss." It is their book, and they read it with the same conviction as that of St. Paul: "This was written for us, who are approaching the end of the ages!" This vision is new. It transforms the content. The Bible continues to be a complicated book with many difficult passages which the people cannot explain. But this attitude to interpreting the Bible is something radically new. It does not derive primarily from our arguments, but from a new experience with the church.

Where the church adopts the option for the poor and the consequent commitment to the struggle against injustice and oppression as the main line of its pastoral activity, that is where we find eyes which can see the biblical message in a new light. The people of the communities which are struggling in practical ways for the liberation of the oppressed discover in the Bible the story of a people like themselves, and discover in God a "partner in the struggle." Once a woman from the interior of Ceará, a state in the north of Brazil, expressed this discovery by saying: "We didn't even need to leave Ceará to understand the Bible!"

Exegetes get to grips with the biblical facts through their studies, the work of their heads. But their bodies do not go along. The people, in contrast, get there with their feet. They tread the same ground of suffering from which the Bible itself sprang. The harsh reality they live today becomes a criterion of interpretation of the ancient text and gives it a sort of connaturality which enables them to grasp the literal sense in its full extent.

Thus the people's freedom in the use of the Bible creates a space in which the Spirit can act, and this is as it should be, since "holy scripture must be read and interpreted in the same Spirit in which it was written" (*Dei Verbum* 12). "And where the Spirit of the Lord is, there is freedom" (2 Cor. 3:17). The Spirit frees us from the prison of the letter which kills and frees the Bible itself, placing it at the side of the little ones who receive from the Father the gift of understanding the message (see Mt. 11:25–26). In this way an ancient truth is rediscovered: the Bible is the book of the church (the community); it is the book of "God's *family.*" Without this broader context of a community involved in the struggle for liberation, the people get lost in the Bible, and the Bible becomes like a voice speaking into a microphone without an amplifier—the richness of the Bible is not amplified, clarified, and deepened in the community engaged in the work of liberation. All this leads us to the third point, summed up in the term "fidelity."

Fidelity

Jesus took the Bible out of the hands of the Pharisees and scribes and started to interpret it in a new way. His different interpretation provoked conflicts. Today, because the Bible is once more in the hands of the people of the communities, it has changed its position and, in a sense, changed class. The fidelity with which the people are beginning to put the word into practice is inconvenient for the rich and powerful and creates conflicts. The people's main interest is not to interpret the Bible, but to interpret life with the help of the Bible. They try to be faithful, not primarily to the meaning the text has in itself (the historical and literal meaning), but to the meaning they discover in the text for their own lives. The growing interest in the literal meaning grows out of the concern to reinforce or criticize the meaning they have discovered in the Bible for their lives and struggles.

For example, a group of around one hundred farmers listed the following topics for detailed discussion in a Bible study:

1. Are the projects we do in the community something the priests have dreamed up, are they communism, or are they from the Bible?

2. Does political education have anything to do with religion and the Bible?

3. Does the campaign for land we're carrying on have a basis in the Bible?

4. Why is it that the drought, when it comes, brings wealth only to the rich and suffering for the poor?

5. One priest reads the Bible in a way which encourages the people, and another priest reads the same Bible in a way which justifies the rich. Which of the two is right?

6. Should Christians be active in the union?

7. Does the gospel have to do only with praying?

8. There is a slave catechism which the owners used to teach us. Today we use the freedom catechism. The owners are against us. What do we do to defend ourselves?

9. At the celebration of the word should we talk only about things to do with God, or should we talk as well about the things we're doing to improve people's lives?

During the meeting the farmers themselves made the distinction between the *written Bible* and the *Bible of life.* The Bible of life was their lives, in which they tried to put into practice and incarnate the word of God. And it was even more: life itself is for them the place where God speaks.

During that meeting the Bible attained its objective and disappeared like salt in food. All that was left was the food spiced by the salt of God's word.

These three points, *freedom, familiarity,* and *fidelity,* sum up the attitude toward interpretation which the people of the communities are adopting toward the Bible. It is just a beginning, a little seed which has fallen on the ground, but which holds promise for the future because it comes from tested stock and has in the church's past ample confirmation of its authenticity. These three qualities are not separate things. They are combined together like coffee, milk, and sugar in the same cup: each influences the taste of the other.

SOME PROBLEMS

Everything new brings problems and conflicts. There are basic ecclesial communities in which no one can read. This situation is a challenge to creativity. Here the traditional methods of literary analysis are not suitable. The people invent others: theater, songs, role-play, group discussion, and so on. The method used in the groups is free association. One idea brings up another. But as the novelty of the initial discovery passes, there is a growing interest in the historical situation of ordinary people in biblical times. People want to know what sort of class divisions there were, and the material conditions of the people Jesus talked to. In this connection the materialist reading of the Bible is a great help. Courses with this basis have multiplied. But on the whole, more scientific exegesis is being questioned by the people in the basic ecclesial communities, who have taken the Bible back into their own hands, and are asking for advice directed not to the problems raised by exegetes, but to the problems raised by the people's own situation. In many places one finds a great thirst for the word of God. It springs from the desire to deepen in the light of faith the struggle for the people's liberation.

Despite all its failings and uncertainties, the people's interpretation of the Bible is making an important contribution to exegesis itself. This contribution has to do with the directness and clarity of the people's vision. The people have regained the correct vision with which Christians should read and interpret the Bible. This vision, this popular interpretation of the Bible, does not read the Bible through the lens of exegetical scholarship and interpretation and is indeed an alarm signal to exegetes. Exegetes must work to enhance this vision of the people. For too long exegetes have tried to shape and alter the people's vision of the Bible, rather than using that vision as a starting-point. When exegetes and others have managed to throw the people's vision of the Bible out of focus, darkness has fallen upon the living words of the biblical text.

2

The Light Breeze

At the Third Inter-Ecclesial Meeting of Basic Communities, held in João Pessoa, Brazil, something very important happened, as important as the light breeze felt by the prophet Elijah on Mount Horeb.

Elijah was looking for God. He wanted God as a support in his struggle against the ideology of the Canaanite religion which was undermining the people's faith at its base. The battle looked lost in advance: the prophets had been killed, the altars destroyed, and the people thrown back on their alliance with God. Elijah thought he was the only person left to defend God's cause (see 1 Kgs. 19:10). Fearing persecution and close to despair, he journeyed to Mount Horeb to replenish his faith at the place where God, through Moses, had sealed the alliance with the people. God had been revealed to Moses in storm, earthquake, and fire (Ex. 19:16–18). Elijah went there to renew contact with this God. And God was there. But God was present in a different form than Elijah had expected. As in Moses' day, there was an earthquake, a storm, and fire, but—so the Bible says—God was not in the earthquake; God was not in the storm; God was not in the fire. Then there was a light breeze, a shift in the wind, hardly noticeable, and Elijah covered his face with his cloak, indicating that he recognized the presence of God. The moral of the story: anyone who looks for God using only the traditional criteria of earthquake, storm, and fire will not find God. The prophet had to change his criteria. The moment of the light breeze was the moment of the great encounter which demanded

Elijah's conversion if he was to discover God's call and face up to his new mission (see 1 Kgs. 19:10–13).

In the João Pessoa meeting, there was, I think, a light breeze, a shift in the wind, a new way in which God's presence was revealed. In this chapter I shall explore the events, the people, and the words of the meeting, looking for the light breeze. The theme will be the way the Bible is being read and interpreted within the church which is being renewed. It is always said that the Bible has to be read and interpreted in accordance with the meaning the church gives it. Well, the meaning given to the Bible by the church which is being born from the people is surprising, a real shift, which deserves to be called "a new reading of the Bible."

I shall not follow the course of events in chronological order, but as they stayed in my memory.

The chapter has three parts. First I shall describe what I discovered during the meeting about the people's reading of the Bible. Then I shall compare those discoveries with some things I have learned about the history of biblical interpretation in the church. The conclusion will argue that the people's interpretation of the Bible seems to be a new fruit from a very old tree, which was once regarded as dead and forgotten, but which has now come back to life.

A NEW READING OF THE BIBLE

The People's Reading of the Bible during the Meeting

THE SITUATION (THE PRE-TEXT)

The meeting began with group sessions in which all persons told the others in their group the situation of their community and described in great detail the suffering of their people. There were people from every corner of Brazil. From north to south, from east to west, the main theme was the exploitation which united them all in the same suffering. The rich exploited the poor, in agriculture, in the factories, in trade, in politics. It is a real "captivity," maintained by the powerful, who are unwilling to lose the source of their income in the labor of the poor.

Next, each person described what his or her people were

doing to free themselves from this "captivity." An Indian spoke of his people's battles against landowners and land-grabbers. His stories were impressively detailed. At one point he said, "It's very difficult to pacify white people because they only want to kill and buy land. They only want money. They bring disease." Out of the family of this Indian, a Xavante chief, his father, mother, more than four brothers and sisters, and various cousins had died as a result of diseases brought by whites or armed struggles waged by the whites against the Indians. In everything he said he brought in his faith in God and in Jesus Christ.

The farmers talked about their conditions. Deprived of almost everything and unable to defend themselves against the exploiters, they were forced to submit to the most terrible conditions in order not to starve. Incredible stories were told of oppression and violence against the poor. It was this desperate situation which made the farmers unite in the struggle to obtain their right to a secure plot of land which would allow them to escape from slavery.

The workers spoke of the various forms of oppression in the factories and of the cry of their people. They described their desire to throw off this harsh slavery. They regarded recent strikes in São Paulo as a victory containing a promise: united, they could win their rights. In these strikes, in which thousands of workers had taken part, there was no mention of God or religion. In this type of struggle what works and is effective is the correct analysis of the situation, political sense, organization, and iron discipline on the part of all around the same plan of action.

In all these cases the motivation for the struggle does not come from the top, from an imposed religion, from priests or bishops; it comes from below, from the intolerable situation in which the people live. The first question you ask other people is not whether they believe in Christ, but whether they are in solidarity with the oppressed. And when one man said during the meeting that what united people in the struggle was not primarily having the same religion (he was Presbyterian), but the common effort of all to improve conditions for ordinary people, he was warmly applauded.

LIVING THE FAITH IN THE COMMUNITY (THE CONTEXT)

The fact that some engaged in the struggle are Christians does not separate them from those who are not Christians. On the contrary, it commits them even more to the one struggle for the liberation of the people. In a sense being a Christian makes the Indian more of an Indian, makes the farmer more supportive of farmers, and makes the worker feel more committed to his or her class.

In the discussions during the meeting there was little reference to the Bible, but on various occasions the word of God could be seen to be the hidden motor powering everything, and it was clear that faith in Christ deepened the participants' commitment to the oppressed people, and that faith and life were mixed in a unity, with faith at the service of life. A farmer, one of the most active members of his union, said, "If it wasn't for the gospel, I wouldn't be here and I wouldn't have the strength to do what I do." The worker who had made the welcoming speech at the beginning of the meeting spoke about his struggle, and in everything he said he used words and events from the gospel and affirmed his faith in the presence and power of the Holy Spirit.

THE "PLACE" FROM WHICH THE PEOPLE READ THE BIBLE: THE GROWTH OF A NEW WAY OF SEEING

All I have just been saying about the pre-text and the context describes the "locus," the place from which the people present at the meeting read and interpret the Bible. This "place" has the following features: (1) It is a situation of "captivity." (2) It is a journey and a struggle in search of liberation. (3) Life and faith are combined in a unity. (4) Faith is at the service of a life being liberated. (5) The Bible is read to nourish this faith which is service.

Now, when the people, living in this "place," begin to interpret the Bible, they explain it with a new vision derived from the "captivity" in which they live and the struggle they wage. In their interpretation the Bible has changed places and gone over to the oppressed.

During the meeting someone described the following incident. On one occasion a worker was commenting on a particular text of the gospel and another man said, "Hey, you've read that bit and drawn your conclusion. The other day in church I heard a priest, who's even taught at the university, read the same bit and draw a conclusion exactly the opposite of what you said. How can that be?" The worker replied with complete simplicity: "But I'm a worker!"

This rather strange reply gives us the key to understanding the new reading the people are making of the Bible. They read with the vision of oppressed people suffering in "captivity" and fighting to free themselves. Because of this they find in the Bible things which are at the same time obvious and surprising, but which do not often appear in the books of exegetes. Here are some examples of this type of interpretation.

THE MEANING THE PEOPLE DISCOVER IN THE BIBLE (THE TEXT)

During the meeting a woman, closing her eyes and looking into the distance to see the idea forming in her head, commented on the parable of the pearl of great price: "As I see it, the pearl is where the poorest, the lowest, the most despised people are, where there's nothing else, where no one looks for anything. That's where the pearl of the kingdom is."

A worker from São Paulo chose the story of Jethro, Moses' father-in-law, as a reading for the celebration on the third day of the meeting. Jethro advised Moses to decentralize the organization of the people. During lunch I asked the worker why she had chosen that reading. She said, "The priests and bishops need a father-in-law like Jethro because they want to do everything themselves in the church and don't leave room for us!" She was talking about a type of domination which exists even within the church.

A farmer who had helped to draw up a letter addressed to the bishops said, "I think we should write a letter like this. Let's think of the bishops as our parents. We are the children who live far from home and are going to tell them how we live. They don't know much about how we live. And we'll say it all in gospel phrases." When the draft was ready, he said, "Now we have to check whether the gospel quotation is right, because I wrote it from memory." There was a sentence which said, "If you put your hand to the plough and look back, you are not worthy of me." I looked in the gospel and found, "Anyone who puts his hand to the plough and looks back is not worthy of me." He said, "It's better to leave what I put because we're talking to the bishops. At Medellín [the second meeting of the Latin American Episcopal Conference, held in Medellín, Colombia] they put their hands to the plough and now they can't look back. They have to keep going forward."

Reflections on the People's Reading of the Bible

These and many other commentaries may seem pious reflections without much basis. Maybe. But they show the new vision with which the people are beginning to read the Bible, a vision different from that with which the exegete usually explains the Bible. We need to examine this point further and see what call from God is hidden in the people's interpretation and what call is revealed.

THE DIFFERENCE BETWEEN THE PEOPLE'S VISION AND THE EXEGETES'

Most exegetes or interpreters, whether priests or pastoral workers, do not live in the people's "captivity" and do not take an active part in the people's struggle for their liberation. As a result, they do not look at things in the same way as the people do. Like it or not, they are, as it were, in the position of bosses watching their cars being repaired by workers. The bosses may know a great deal of factual data about mechanics that they have learned from manuals and they may have even taught that data to the workers, but, as much as the bosses look at or study the cars, they do not feel or see the same thing as the workers. The workers, lying on the ground on pieces of dirty sacking, wearing oil-soaked overalls, look at the cars, the same cars, from below. And they look at cars which are not theirs and which they cannot own.

The people are looking at the Bible, lying on the ground of life, on the dirty sacking of injustices, wearing clothes soaked in dirt and blood. The difference from the workers repairing the car is that today the people are beginning to look at the Bible as their book. After repairing the cars of thousands of bosses, the people now, finally, are adjusting the plugs on an old car which is their own. We, exegetes or interpreters, priests or pastoral workers, who were always the owners of the Bible and of knowledge about the Bible—we are not capable of having the same vision, the same joy, gratitude, wonder, novelty, and commitment that the people bring to the Bible.

This new way of seeing is growing up within the small basic ecclesial communities which are the heart of the church, since it is in them, gradually, that faith is mingling with the tortured lives of the people to form a single whole. Now we can appreciate the importance of that oft-repeated maxim: "Read the Bible in accordance with the meaning the church gives it." Within the practice of these communities a new vision of the church is coming into being: the church at the service of people. It is this vision of the church which has made the Bible change sides and is placing the Bible in the center of the painful lives of people who live in "captivity" and are struggling to free themselves.

All this is communicated in those very simple commentaries on the pearl, Moses' father-in-law, and the plough. Intellectuals have difficulty producing such commentaries. And even if they succeeded, their commentaries would not have the solidity and life of the discoveries made by the people.

THE RIGHT "PLACE" FOR INTERPRETING THE BIBLE

But someone might object, "So are the exegete's scientific studies suddenly useless? What is the scientific value of these popular commentaries? Is biblical interpretation going to be reduced to these scattered commentaries by the people?" Obviously not. I am not trying to reject the achievements of scientific exegesis, nor to consecrate as right and infallible whatever explanation the people give of the Bible. This is not the problem I am dealing with here. I am trying to map out the place from which the word of God ought to be—is asking to be—read and interpreted by us. I would like to know what the commentaries by the people were which made Jesus say: "I bless you, Father, Lord of heaven and earth, for hiding these things from the learned and the clever and revealing them to these little ones. Yes, Father, for that is what it pleased you to do" (Mt. 11:25–26). Those statements were certainly not prompted by lofty considerations about the historico-literal meaning of texts or the mechanisms of social oppression. The gift the Father gives the "little ones" does not compete with the science of the "learned and clever," but strips science of its supposed neutrality and gives it a new support and a new destiny. And the destiny of the scientists, the exegetes, is not to impose an understanding of the Bible on the "little ones" or to shape or alter their vision of the biblical texts. Rather the exegetes are to be at the service of the poor and their vision of the Bible. The destiny of these "learned and clever" ones is to cooperate with the poor and to clarify, enhance, and sharpen their vision.

Scientific exegesis has already helped to strip away some false preconceptions of the Bible which in the past the learned and powerful had used to distort the way in which the Bible was viewed and understood. For instance, scientific studies have shown clearly that the Bible originated in the people's life of suffering. The Bible was the product of a journey toward liberation. It originated in the lives of those in "captivity" and in the lives of those in solidarity with them. There have always been people who tried to take over and monopolize the Bible in order to use it to justify their own ideas. But it is only within the concrete world of the "captivity" of the poor that we can find the right place from which to discover the true meaning of the Bible. To put it another way, it is only within this hard life the people lead in "captivity" and within this journey toward liberation that we can find a hidden meaning of the Bible which can give a new support and a new goal to the science of exegesis. That is where we find the "little ones" who receive from God the gift of understanding the message of Jesus. And Jesus added these very serious words: "Yes, Father, for that is what it pleased you to do."

And who are these "little ones" Jesus talks about? Clearly they are not the "great." They are not the "learned and clever." They were and still are the poor people deprived of knowledge by the doctors of the law, excluded from power by the power of the great, deprived of their possessions by the profits of the rich. They are the "poor of Yahweh" the prophet Zephaniah talks about: "In your midst I will leave a humble and lowly people [who] will seek refuge in Yahweh" (3:12). They are also those

who, like Zacchaeus, recognize their injustices and say, "I am
going to give half my property to the poor, and if I have cheated
anybody I will pay him back four times the amount" (Lk. 19:8).
And, finally, they are all those who are ready to lose their lives
to find them (see Mt. 16:25).

To understand the meaning of the word of God for us today
science is not enough, however good it may be. We also need
the Spirit of understanding which is a gift of God, given by the
Father to the "little ones." Jesus himself confirms this. If the
professors, exegetes, priests, ministers, or pastoral workers wish
to possess this sight given by the Spirit, they have to do two
things: (1) ask the Father for it in prayer, and (2) become "little"
or be on the side of the "little ones." This was the "position"
Jesus took and from there he spoke to all, without excluding
anyone.

THE TWO RAILS WHICH CARRY THE TRAIN OF INTERPRETATION

In saying the above I have not the slightest desire to diminish
the importance of the contribution of scientific exegesis to biblical interpretation. What I want to do is to complete it. The
people's approach is not the scientific approach which discovers
the historico-literal meaning. Discovering the historico-literal
meaning is the task of exegetes. Thanks to their research, we
can today know, down to the smallest details, the literal meaning
of the biblical texts and the situation of the people of those
bygone times. This relatively new knowledge makes the Bible an
ancient book because it places it in the past, in the situation in
which it originated. This is the first stage in the process of interpretation: discovering the literal meaning, the meaning as such
of the text. This is the base of everything, the root.

But it is not enough to know how the text came into being
and the meaning it had in the past. We have to bring it back
into the present. The science of exegesis in itself cannot bring
the Bible back to the present and tell us the meaning the Spirit
of God is offering the church today by means of this ancient
text. Only the Spirit of God can do that. And the Father shares
this Spirit first with the "little ones." The vision which the "little
ones" receive from the Father is a very ancient vision which
makes the Bible a new and relevant book, because it places it

in the present, in the situation in which the people live today. This is the second stage, which completes the process of interpretation; in the second stage we discover the Spirit's meaning, the meaning-for-us. This is the fruit which grows ultimately from the root.

We have now identified the two strands of biblical interpretation, the study of the "letter" and the action of the Spirit. Both are necessary. They are connected like two rails along which the train of interpretation travels. Without both "rails" interpretation cannot move forward toward a correct understanding of the Bible. The science of exegesis teaches us about the "letter" of the Bible, but it is the Spirit which reveals to us the call of God which is present inside the "letter" (see Jn. 14:26; 16:13). The Pharisees were content with the "letter" alone and closed themselves to the Spirit which revealed itself in Jesus and in the "little ones"; because of this the Pharisees were an obstacle to the liberation of their people. St. Paul learned the lesson and said, "The written letters kill, but the Spirit gives life" (2 Cor. 3:6). However, even guided by the breath of the Spirit, the people on their own, without a critical understanding of the text, are not always able to justify their discoveries by the "letter" of the Bible, that is, in the historico-literal meaning of the texts. Asked about the reason for their interpretation, they reply, "But I'm a worker!" They cannot explain the hope which inspires them (see 1 Pet. 3:15) and run the risk of falling into an alienating spiritualist interpretation.

The Criteria of Biblical Interpretation

How do we maintain the connection between the two "rails," the "letter" and the "Spirit," so that the train of interpretation moves forward in history? At the beginning I said that in interpreting the word of God we need to take account of three factors: the *pre-text* of life, the *context* of the community's faith, and the *text* of the Bible. Each of these factors has its own demands. To discover the demands of the pre-text, we have to use what might be called the criteria of solidarity; to reveal the demands of the context, we need to employ the criteria of the community's or the church's faith; and to discover the demands of the text, we have to use the criteria of scientific exegesis.

In the past in seminaries or in Bible courses there was always great insistence on the use of the criteria of scientific exegesis. There was also a stress, not quite so strong, on the use of faith criteria, almost always understood as the directives of the hierarchy and not as the experience of living the faith in the communities at the base of society. The criteria of solidarity, however, were never strongly recommended. The criteria of solidarity have to do with the "place" in which the interpreter lives and from which he or she starts reading the Bible. The process of interpretation, with its to-and-fro between "letter" and "Spirit," between past and present, between object and subject, never takes place on neutral ground, but in a particular "place" or position, in which life-values and gospel-values have to be defined. The criteria of solidarity enable the interpreter to define a position in relation to the social context, and so to be in the right "place."

In practice these criteria consist of the interpreter's solidarity with the cause of the oppressed, with the "little ones." They entail a critical experience, that is, a familiarity with the mechanisms of oppression in the society in which we live. The interpreter has to have a critical view, not just of the biblical text, but also of the pretext, that is, of our current reality.

These criteria of experience help us to overcome the division between life and the Bible, science and faith, "letter" and "Spirit." When these criteria are allowed to occupy their proper place in the process of interpretation, they bring the interpreter to conversion, to a change of position, so that he or she begins to use the lamp of faith and the instruments of science in the service of the liberation of the "little ones" who live in "captivity."

The Light Breeze

POLITICS AND FAITH

During the meeting, I was reminded in numerous conversations of the enormous importance of the Bible for the life and liberative activity of the church which has grown out of the people. But what was really striking was that it was precisely the people most concerned with the political dimension of faith who most insisted on the importance and necessity of the ministry of the word for the life of the communities, that is, the need to stress the religious dimension of political activity to make it really liberative.

I had come to the meeting thinking that there would be a lot of tension between the champions of a more political line and those who insisted more on the need for faith. The tension existed, but in a different form from what I had imagined. It was not a case of one side wanting to bring the other to its point of view, but of both wanting to put their ideas at the service of the people suffering in "captivity." Those who argued for a more political position admitted, "Political action alone won't bring the people to the total liberation God is offering us. We must stress that even political action has a faith dimension." Those who insisted more on the need for faith recognized, "The Bible and faith on their own won't bring the people to the total liberation God is offering us. We have to insist that even faith has a political dimension." Faith and politics converged in a desire to serve the people, and both sides were ready to learn from each other and from the people in order to bring about the liberation of all in accordance with God's plan.

CHANGING PLACES

In connection with all this, another thought came to me: the church is no longer the center of history. The people's history has become independent and follows its own course, even without the church. Nevertheless the church is being invited, insistently, to enter into the people's history and offer its help. It is an invitation from God, the Lord of history, the creator of the people, who speaks not only through the Bible, but also through the events of history.

In this way I came to see the importance of the Bible, not from the Bible itself, nor from the ideas I acquired from my education, but from the people clamoring for justice. It is not the Bible which pleads, "Defend me from the world because I'm very important for you Christians." It is the world, wanting fellowship and justice, which says, "Defend the Bible and show me its value, because I can see from the lives of the people who believe in it that it's very important for me."

In both cases we are asked to defend the Bible, but there is a great difference. In the first case we are defending the Bible for its own sake, defending it in order to have it for ourselves. In the second case we are defending the Bible for the sake of the people's welfare, defending it in order to give better service to others. Within the Bible itself we can find the same thing. God too defends the divine prerogative and never allows anyone to claim the honor due to God alone. But it is never for God's own sake. If God defends what is divine, it is for the sake of the people. God knows that without God the people will never attain full liberation. In the same way the Bible does not need defending for its own sake. But it has to be defended for the sake of the people who need it to bring their journey toward liberation to a successful conclusion.

But how does the Bible have to be defended, and against whom? The best defense of the Bible is to do everything possible to ensure that it is always in the "place" where God wants it to be, that is, alongside the oppressed people, the "little ones," but open to all. It has to be defended against all those who want to move it from this "place." And in order to defend it the church must use all the power it possesses.

The "light breeze" of the Spirit which blew during the meeting is a rejuvenating breeze blowing also through the church and through the institutions where the Bible is studied and interpreted. This breeze is prompting more and more people to the following discovery: the real importance of the Bible is revealed, not by the Bible itself, nor by the traditional criteria, but by the journey of the people trying to escape from "captivity" into the freedom God promises them. This changes the whole emphasis of interpretation. The moment of the light breeze was the moment of the great meeting in which God asked even the prophet Elijah to be humble and be converted. God asks much more of us, who are not great prophets like Elijah.

HOW THE FATHERS OF THE CHURCH READ THE BIBLE

Most people know little about the "spiritual exegesis" practiced by the Fathers of the Church. Like the people's commentaries taken in isolation, it gives the impression of being an arbitrary exegesis which owes more to imagination than to critical reason. This judgment, however, is superficial and does not go to the heart of the matter. When leaves yellow and fall, we do not have to conclude that the tree is dead. It can also be a sign of life and the promise of a future spring. The study which follows of the ancient leaves that have now turned yellow or fallen has only one purpose: to recover the criterion which will enable us to recognize the new leaves which are bursting out today from every branch of this old tree. Memory does not preserve the past as something over and done with, but as a living force which moves the present on toward the future. The real past has not remained in the past. It is the basis of the present.

"Letter" and "Spirit": The Fathers' Spiritual Exegesis

THE STARTING-POINT: THE "LETTER" AND "HISTORY"

As regards their biblical exegesis, the Fathers of the Church are sometimes falsely accused of ignoring history and the literal meaning and fantasizing without any basis in the texts. This is not true. Their own premise was that all interpretation must start from the "letter" and from "history." For them "letter" and "history" are synonyms, denoting the things that really happened and can be verified by human science.

Nevertheless the very fact that they say, "First we must investigate the letter," itself shows that the letter is not the final goal. The Fathers believed that merely to explain the letter and the history of the Bible, that is, with a concern limited to the historico-literal meaning, is to stop at the door of the Bible without entering. The letter, they say, is like the body which sustains the invisible soul. Without the soul the body is worth little, but we have to study the body carefully in order to understand the soul.

Once the literal meaning has been determined the real work begins: that is, discovering its significance. This will now have a solid basis in the letter and will not be a product of imagination. To work from the other end, says St. Augustine, would leave the significance hanging like a castle in the air.

The Aim: To Get behind the "Letter" to the "Spirit" within

Why did the Fathers want to go beyond the letter and history? And what is this significance, which they also call the "spiritual meaning"? They appeal to St. Paul's saying, "The written letters kill, but the Spirit gives life" (2 Cor. 3:6). To go no further than the letter of the Bible, the facts and the texts, without looking for what lies beyond, behind, or within them, that is, without looking for the pointers to Christ and to the community living its faith today, would be what the Fathers called a "Jewish interpretation" of the Bible. The Jews went no further than the letter, without asking about its fulfilment in Christ (see 2 Cor. 3:13–14).

The Fathers frequently use the terms "image," "figure," "type," and "shadow" when referring to the Old Testament. The comparison with a shadow is illuminating. When I see a shadow approaching, I wait to see the person who is casting it in front of him or her. Once the person has appeared, this gives me a key to understand all the details of the shadow. Before the person arrives, the shadow remains wrapped in mystery and does not reveal all its secrets. The person in this case is Christ.

For the Jews the history of the Old Testament was not the shadow of Christ, but reality itself. Because of this they did not look beyond the shadow; they remained trapped in the "letter" and became incapable of understanding their own history (see 2 Cor. 3:13). For the Christians, because they had received the Spirit of Christ, the history of the Old Testament was the shadow which Christ cast in front of him and which proclaimed his coming in the future. Because of this the whole of the Old Testament became for them an image or figure of Christ, of the church, and of the Christian living his or her faith in the present. In this "shadow" everything had to have some relationship with the Christian life, since "all these things . . . were described in writing to be a lesson for us, to whom it has fallen to live in the last days of the ages" (1 Cor. 10:11).

When the Fathers say that they want to go beyond the letter and history to get to the Spirit within them, what they are trying to do is to elucidate this basic movement in the Old Testament toward Christ and toward the church. They are trying to insert the ancient text into the new context of the Christian community's life of faith. They want to make the text speak to Christians. Through this spiritual interpretation they are trying to discover the Bible's meaning-for-us, that is, the meaning which God is revealing to us today, through the Holy Spirit, by means of the ancient text of the Bible.

This type of interpretation, which treats the Bible not just as *history,* but also as a *mirror* — in which Christians discover something of themselves, of their experience, and of their ideals — is not just the result of intelligence applied to the text. It is, first and foremost, an event, a discovery, a *revelation,* in the precise sense of the term: a pulling back of the veil which covers the meaning. It is not just the product of calculations and studies, but also a gift received through faith in the resurrection. It does not spring from the text only, but also from the Spirit acting in the vision of the person who reads the text.

Opposition and Continuity between "Letter" and "Spirit"

For us today the literal meaning of the Bible is the meaning the sacred authors wanted to convey through their words to their readers. The instrument we use to discover this meaning is scientific exegesis. Our perspective is literary. The perspective of the Fathers was different. For them the literal meaning, or the "letter," as they called it, was the information conveyed by the Old Testament facts when analyzed in themselves, without their reference to Christ and the church. It was for this very reason that they refused to be content with the "letter" — they believed that reality cannot be explained solely in its own terms; reality can be fully understood only in reference to the destiny it has been given by the creator. Their great concern was to go beyond the "letter" and discover within it the "Spirit," that is, the destined fulfilment in Christ.

Consequently the opposition and the continuity which the Fathers set up in this way between "letter" and "Spirit," that is, between Old and New Testament, are much more than a chronological opposition and continuity between two successive periods. They are also, and primarily, a permanent opposition and continuity between two states of faith, different and contemporaneous, each in tension with the other. In our own terms it would be the opposition and continuity between nature and grace, between science and faith, between humanism and Christianity, between secular history and the history of salvation, between human development and evangelization, between socio-economic liberation and liberation from sin, between politics and mysticism, between the horizontal approach and the vertical approach, between the world and the kingdom of God, between, as St. Paul puts it, the old human being and the new human being. These are *our* two testaments. The Old Testament exists to flow into the New and to be criticized and completed by it. The New finds in the Old its basis and its preparation.

The opposition becomes a break and a discontinuity when the first, the Old, closes in on itself and tries to reduce the other, the New, to the dimensions of the Old; when the first makes itself an absolute and no longer recognizes in the other a possibility of correction and fulfilment; or when the second minimizes the first and does not recognize in it its own preparation, its starting-point, and its basis, and denies it any value. We destroy the unity of God's plan if we applaud the gospel only when it confirms our ideas, whether progressive or conservative, and reject it when it criticizes or condemns them. We also destroy the unity of God's plan if we ignore human struggles and aspirations and imprison ourselves in ideas picked up in the gospel alone.

The Fathers never had this closed attitude — they followed neither a humanism closed in on itself nor a spiritualism which denied the value of the human. They systematically refused to be content with the "letter" alone. They also rejected the interpretation which only sought the "Spirit," without any basis in the "letter." They wanted both, "letter" and "Spirit." In our terms this would be: science *and* faith, socio-economic liberation *and* liberation from sin, politics *and* mysticism. Though "letter" and "Spirit" are distinct entities, they are not parallel and separate entities. They exist united within real life, like body and soul, indivisible. Though there exists a tension between the two, they are not in competition. The competition and the separation appear where there is an erroneous or defective vision of what "letter" and "Spirit" are. The one does not threaten the other. The tension between the two is not a force for division but for convergence. The destiny of both is to achieve unity in the service of God's plan. Interpretation is at the service of this unity. It attempts to elucidate the critique and the fulfilment which the "Spirit" brings to the "letter."

The Basis of the Connection between "Letter" and "Spirit"

THE CONTINUITY AND OPPOSITION BETWEEN CREATION AND SALVATION

The Fathers' attitude to interpretation made its entry into history when the first Christians, motivated by their desire to reveal Christ to the Jews, began to "re-read" the Old Testament in the light of their faith in the resurrection. It arose as *pastoral practice*. It did not come from a previously worked out theory.

When they carried out this "re-reading" of the Old Testament, the Christians discovered that the gold they had found in the subsoil of Jewish history was also present in the subsoil of every people's history. *Pastoral practice* thus helped unearth the "gold" that was buried in the lives of all human beings and peoples. In this way pastoral practice led to the development of the basic structure of the quite particular vision which Christians bring to life, history, and the Bible, that is, the vision that everything was created by God to find its full realization in Christ.

Faith teaches us not only that God saves us with a *creative* power, but also that God *created* us to save us in Christ. There is a real continuity between the work of creation and the work of salvation. A single plan includes both. Creation, that is, nature, life, history, facts, all human reality, everything that human beings do and produce for their good, the meaning-in-itself of things, the "letter," as the Fathers used to say, all that touches us closely—all these have a destiny and a direction which go beyond them and which derive from the creator's intention to save everything and everyone in Christ (see Eph. 1:9–10).

In the perspective of this broader *context* which faith opens up on the world, "letter" and "Spirit" are no longer qualities exclusive to the Bible. On the contrary, they are dimensions of reality as such. It is because they are *universal* dimensions of reality that they *also* exist in the Bible. All human life has its "letter," *within which* the "Spirit" acts to give it a new meaning. Everything has a meaning-in-itself (the literal meaning), which human beings discover by applying their intelligence and the instruments of their science, and a meaning-for-us (the spiritual meaning), which we receive from our faith and which concerns the direction to be given to the meaning-in-itself of things and life.

Just like the Old Testament, the *whole* of human life can be analyzed in two ways: as *sola littera,* that is, in terms of the data of the situation analyzed in itself, without reference to Christ; or as *littera et allegoria,* that is, not closed in on itself, but open to a further meaning, from which it receives its direction, correction, and fulfilment. Like the Jews, we all run the risk of imprisoning ourselves in the "written letters which kill" (2 Cor. 3:6). This is true both of the exegetes who imprison themselves inside the analysis of the ancient text's meaning-in-itself and of all others who make science absolute and exclude anything beyond the range of their scientific methods.

The two aspects of Christian interpretation, which derive from the demands of the "letter" (the meaning-in-itself) and from the "Spirit" (the meaning-for-us), form a unity which originates not in a human whim but in God's unique plan. The basis of this exegesis which refuses to stop at the "letter," but wants to transcend it to reach the "Spirit" within, is the continuity which exists between the creative and the saving word of God. When we try to combine the search for the meaning-in-itself and the search for the meaning-for-us, we are not trying to combine two things which were never connected, but we are attempting to reconcile what was once separated by Adam's sin. For the Christian interpreter the "letter" (that is, history, life, events, and all things) is, as it were, pregnant with the Spirit. With this "spiritual" exegesis, Christians attempt to hasten the delivery so that the world might rejoice at the birth of a new dimension which has appeared in human life with Christ.

GOD'S MESSAGE THROUGH CREATION AND THE BIBLE

"Without sin, the world would have been an adequate symbol in its unchanged transparency; but now we need the help of scripture to understand it." This statement sums up many other remarks of the Fathers, and shows that they saw an intrinsic relationship between the world and scripture, life and faith. The

Bible was given to us to help us to discover the meaning of life. Its function is to transform the dark glass of human life into transparent glass, so that the presence of God, there from the beginning, might show through once more.

Henri de Lubac, using phrases from the Fathers, notably St. Augustine, expressed the idea as follows:

> Now the fabric of the world has become completely opaque. It only reveals its meaning after much mental effort and patience on our part. We need another, clearer book as a commentary on the first. Because of this, the Holy Spirit, the finger of God, who had already written the letters of the creation, set to work to compose this new book and spread over us the sky of the scriptures. They are like new heavens, which, like the first, declare the power of God and, more strongly than the first, sing of his mercy. Thanks to them the faculty of contemplation has been restored to us, and the whole of creation thus becomes for us a theophany, a revelation of God.

In other words, God has written two books, the book of life and the book of faith. The second has no purpose in itself, but exists in function of the first, in that it provides a *commentary* on its content, helps us to decipher what is unintelligible in it, and restores to those who study it the *faculty of contemplation.*

Another striking phrase runs: "Scripture explains what creation puts before us." It is like an art exhibition, where the visitor receives a catalogue which explains the works on display. The Bible is the catalogue of the world which Christians receive from its creator so that they can understand the various elements of life and so give real service to this life. An exhibition without a catalogue leaves visitors disoriented. The catalogue without the exhibition is just an absurdity.

The vision resulting from a comparison of the two books puts the Bible in its proper place and condemns any sort of Biblicism, scientific or otherwise, which imprisons itself in the study of the historico-literal meaning and does not bring that meaning into our world. It also condemns an excessive veneration of the Bible, as though it alone could bring salvation.

The Bible exists only in function of life, to enable life to speak to us once more about God, the living and true God, the liberator from the beginning. This ancient vision is the "criterion of faith" which should give direction to all the scientific work of Christian interpretation. All the disciplines which go into the interpretation of the Bible must constantly face this purpose of the Bible and let themselves be corrected by it. Even if the discipline of exegesis in the strict sense is determined and defined by the search for the historico-literal meaning, the purpose of the Bible must influence the means and methods used in the discovery of this meaning. If a car is designed to be used on dirt roads, this has to be borne in mind from the first moment of its manufacture. The manufacturer cannot say, "That's the driver's problem. Let her sort it out!" Equally, if the Bible exists "for us who are approaching the end of the ages," if its purpose is to make life transparent, then this purpose must be borne in mind from the first moment of its interpretation. The interpreter cannot just say, "That's a problem for the parish priest and the catechist. Let them sort it out!" The exegete is not the owner of God's word, just an interpreter.

The Two Functions of the Bible and the Two Aspects of Interpretation

Insofar as the *history* of the Hebrew people fulfilled God's plan and reached resurrection in Christ, it has become *exemplary,* that is, it has become a mirror, a model capable of revealing the basic meaning of human existence. As a model or normative experience, it is able "to make plain to all a knowledge of God and of human beings and of the ways in which the just and merciful God deals with human beings" (*Dei Verbum*).

Thus the Bible, which describes this history for us, has two functions: (1) to *inform* us about what God has done and taught in the past, and (2) by means of this information, and building on it, to *reveal* to those who believe in the resurrection the signs of the presence and liberative action of this same God in the life and history of people alive today.

As a result of these two functions of the Bible, exegesis — including that of the Fathers, as we have seen — has two aspects:

it searches for the "history" (the "letter") and for the exemplary content (the "Spirit"). Each of the functions of the Bible and each of the attendant aspects of interpretation are equally important and inseparably linked. They are the root and fruit of the same tree. A systematic summary of these two functions and aspects may clarify matters more and put us in a better position to understand the use the people make of the Bible.

To Reveal: The Normative or Exemplary Aspect

As a model, the Bible has, for those who believe in the resurrection, the authority and inspiration to reveal to us who God is, who we are, what God has to say to us, how God is present in our lives and history, and how God is guiding us through the Spirit toward Christ and the resurrection. To put it another way, as a model, the Bible reveals a hidden dimension of human life which cannot be seen by the naked eye, by science alone, but is nonetheless real for all that. This dimension has to do with the liberating presence of God in human life. The Bible arouses in Christians the desire to search, and places us in a process of searching. It helps us to discover, within our own lives and history, this reality of the liberating presence of God.

In order to be able to discover this meaning the Bible has *for us,* people must have faith in the resurrection, live in the community (church), and from it receive the Spirit of Christ which removes the veil (see 2 Cor. 3:16–17). The "letter" alone, the meaning-in-itself, closed in on itself, is incapable of revealing all that is in the Bible. The "letter" *informs* us that God is present, but it is the Spirit who *reveals* God as present. The Spirit gives life to the information provided by the "letter."

Now the investigation or the appropriation of this *exemplary* character of the Bible for human life gave rise, and still gives rise, to a particular attitude toward interpretation among Christians. For a period this took the form of the so-called allegorical-spiritual exegesis of the Fathers. Trusting in the promise of Christ that the Spirit would lead them into the full understanding of the truth (see Jn. 14:26; 16:13), Christians never ceased, nor ever will, to look for "the fruits of the Spirit beneath the pages of the letter" (St. Jerome). The method may change, and must change, but the basic attitude of faith does not change and keeps on reappearing. It has reappeared in our time in the interpretation the Christian people are making of the Bible. An *ancient* vision is making the Bible a *new* book because it is placing it in the present, where the people live.

TO INFORM: THE HISTORICAL ASPECT

As *history,* the Bible informs us about the long journey made by the Hebrew people which finally brought us the savior and the promised gift of the Spirit. It shows, in the detail of a people's history, how the action of the Spirit and the Word of God stamped a new meaning on human existence through the resurrection of Christ. As an account of things, facts, and statements which really occurred, the "letter" of the Bible thus gives us the basis of the faith we possess and justifies the *exemplary* or *spiritual* use we make of it.

Attacks on the faith are usually directed not at the exemplary use of the Bible, but at its historical basis. The attacks try to criticize, undermine, or improve the "letter" (or "history") which is at the root of the spiritual or normative reading of the Bible, because the "letter" is an object of human investigation and is within the range of science's critical eye. For this reason a new critical reading of the "letter" usually provokes a crisis in the "spiritual" reading of the Bible. This happened at the beginning of this century when historical and linguistic disciplines began to be used to elucidate the literal meaning. It is happening today as the social sciences and even historical materialism are brought to bear on the "letter" of the Bible.

The need to have a solid basis for a "spiritual" or exemplary reading, corresponding with the demands of faith in the given historical moment, leads Christians of all ages to investigate the "letter" and the "history." They want to demonstrate to others and to themselves that their attitude of faith is not an illusion, but a rational attitude with a firm basis in a history which really took place. This concern with the basis of faith was present at the origin of the Bible itself. St. Luke, for example, collected in his gospel the facts of Jesus' life, so that the reader could "learn how well-founded the teaching is that you have received" (Lk. 1:4). St. Peter recommends that Christians should always be ready to give reason for the hope within them (1 Pet. 3:15).

So the investigation or the use of the *historical* aspect of the Bible has always produced, and is still producing, a distinct attitude toward interpretation, which currently takes the form of so-called historico-literal exegesis. This arises out of love for truth, out of the conviction that faith is not an illusion, and out of the desire to be assured "how well-founded the teaching is that you have received."

THE CURRENT TENSION BETWEEN THE TWO ASPECTS OF INTERPRETATION

We have seen the two aspects of Christian interpretation of the Bible — that is, the search for the historical, the "letter," and for the exemplary, the "Spirit" — applied in the exegesis of the Fathers. Today there is a great tension between the two aspects, resulting from the emphasis on science in the investigation of the "letter."

The more critical interpretation of the "letter" resulting from the use of scientific methods began outside the Catholic Church and produced a crisis in the "spiritual" interpretation of the Bible which the church had hitherto been offering. Many traditional practices, attitudes, doctrines, and customs were questioned. The very historical basis of the faith seemed in danger. Under pressure from the situation and with the encouragement of the magisterium, exegetes went into the field to challenge the accusations and reinforce the defense of the "letter" as real history. In order to mount an effective defense they had to use the same weapons which were being used against them. In this regard Pope Pius XII proposed an ideal that exegetes should keep in mind when they use science to investigate the meaning of the Bible. He wrote that "interpreters of today" should seek to bring about "the happy and fruitful union between the doctrine and spiritual sweetness of expression of the ancient authors and the greater erudition and mature knowledge of the modern, having as its result new progress in the never fully explored and inexhaustible field of divine letters" (*Divino Afflante Spiritu* 17).

But concern with the "letter," with the literal meaning, became so absorbing and took on such huge proportions, that the purpose of the interpretation, that is, to give the people the meaning-for-us, slipped off the exegetes' agenda. The status of the Bible as a normative example became an "extrinsic and additional" appendix to biblical interpretation. While scientific exegesis progressed, the method of spiritual exegesis was not modernized, and remained imprisoned in the forms inherited from the past and thus fell into disrepute. As the method became discredited, spiritual exegesis itself became suspect as not obeying scientific criteria. The "happy and fruitful union" of the ancient vision and modern science desired by Pius XII has still not been achieved. The "letter" has won. The scientist has developed; the believer has remained stunted.

Today it is the people who are calling for the integration of these two aspects of biblical interpretation. The people are not satisfied with a mere exposition of the historico-literal meaning. They want to find the meaning which the literal meaning has for them today, in the situation in which they live. They are already taking their own initiatives, often without any formation in the "letter" and the "history." Under the pressure of this pastoral need, Pope Paul VI shared his concern with Italian exegetes when he said:

Interpretation will not have completed its task until it has shown how the meaning of scripture can be related to the present moment of salvation, that is, when it demonstrates its application in the current situation of the church and the world.

And later in the same address he said:

Fidelity to the Incarnate Word also requires, in virtue of the dynamic of the incarnation, that the message be made present, in its entirety, not to people in general, but to the men and women of today, those to whom the message is now being proclaimed. Christ became the contemporary of a particular group of people and spoke their language. Fidelity to him demands that this contemporaneous continue. This is the whole mission of the church, with its tradition, its magisterium and its preaching. Exegetes must contribute to this task. Fidelity to the people of today is difficult and demands effort, but it is necessary if we are

to remain totally faithful to the message [in *Acta Aposto-
licae Sedis* 62 (1970), pp. 615–18].

The challenge presented here is a new one. Scientific exegesis
has become independent and autonomous, and is guided by its
own principles. How can we ensure that it serves faith and helps
us to discover the "spiritual" meaning, without losing any of its
autonomy and without returning to a prescientific stage? How
are we to ensure that scientific exegesis itself can be enriched
by "the doctrine and spiritual sweetness of expression of the
ancient authors" referred to by Pius XII? How can we put an
exegesis which is so advanced and often so sophisticated at the
service of our people, who live by the simple faith they received
from their parents? How can we persuade exegetes, so accus-
tomed to the principles of their science, that they have to become students of these simple people and learn from them the
right way to look at the Bible?

This is the tension which is today running through not just
exegesis, but also other areas of the church's life. It appeared
in the João Pessoa meeting, in a propitious and promising form,
as a tension between faith and politics. It is a constructive, not
a destructive, tension.

The Basic Structure of Christian Interpretation of the Bible and Life

THE BIBLE AWAKENS THE MEMORY OF LIFE

I want to use an illustration in an attempt to show the basic
structure of the interpretative attitude with which the Christian
approaches the Bible and life.

When I talk about my friend's face, and describe his features
one by one, I may give the impression that I am talking about
things which apply to many people: blue eyes, brown hair, mus-
tache, beard, and so on. There is nothing easier than to describe,
one by one, the features of a face. There is nothing more difficult
than to convey, through a description, the particular and unmistakable image of my friend's face. If the persons to whom I
am trying to describe my friend do not know the face, and have
never met my friend, no description is adequate. They are not

going to be able to re-create within themselves the particular, unmistakable image of the face that I am trying to communicate. They have to have seen the face, at least once, for my description to awaken their memory and perhaps call up the pleasure they felt in that first meeting, and arouse the desire to renew and deepen the acquaintance with this friend. In this case the description I give receives life and meaning from the memory and the pleasure it awakens in these other persons.

The Christian interpretation of the Bible starts from the premise—which is gratuitous and derives from faith but is not proved by science—that there has been an initial meeting between human beings and God. Created by God and for God, the human race carries within itself the mark of God, feels a longing for its Origin and an attraction toward its End, though it is unable to define either exactly, since it no longer remembers them. This memory is asleep in the depths of consciousness, waiting for someone with the power to awaken it and, finally, release its repressed force.

The history of the Old Testament is the history of the recovery of this memory which finally awakened completely in the resurrection of Christ. St. Paul put it as follows: "[Christ] is the image of the unseen God, the first-born of all creation; for in him were created all things. . . . All things were created through him and for him. He exists before all things, and in him all things hold together" (Col. 1:15–16, 17). The description of this history, preserved in the Bible, and its interpretation are intended to awaken in us the memory of life.

The interpreter describes, one by one, the features of the face of God which appear in the Bible. He or she uses the science of exegesis for this, and proceeds with maximum rigor, to avoid any confusion with false gods. The purpose of this description is to call up from the depths of people's memory the longing left there by the first meeting and to transform it into hope and assurance that another meeting is possible. It is the longing and the memory, awakened in this way among the people, which will give the interpreter's description its true meaning. Unless it awakens something in the people, the information the interpreter provides will remain a dead "letter," lifeless. It is the Spirit of Christ, by awakening the memory of the people, which gives life to the "letter" and the explanation of it.

Accordingly, in any really Christian interpretation, the people do not encounter, cannot encounter, something totally strange and unknown. On the contrary, they should be able to encounter in it the unexpected formulation of their deepest aspirations, the undeserved restoration of their lost hope, the good news of God which restores their identity as people and the awareness of their mission. The great challenge for an interpreter is this: to present the features of the face which appears in the Bible in such a way that it can awaken today in the people a longing and memory. This requires that interpreters remain close to the people to whom they seek to explain the Bible.

SPEEDING HISTORY TOWARD THE DEFINITIVE ENCOUNTER WITH GOD

The facts of our life are like features on a torn painting, fragmented, mixed up, and not making much sense. The face imprinted on it on the day of creation has been disfigured. No one has ever seen this face, since the painting was already torn when we were born. But it exists. It is still possible to see certain features of that face, though torn and lost, and occasionally to glimpse something of their beauty and attractiveness. We catch sight of them, for example, in an act of kindness, in a death suffered for others, in the simplicity of the people's attitudes — their love of truth, their dedication to life, their solidarity — and in a prayer or a friendly embrace, in a great love or a terrible pain, in silence, or even in the midst of the city's noise. Infinite possibilities! Features of a face so beautiful — even though torn and defiled — as to provoke in the soul an irresistible nostalgia.

The story of the Bible is the story of how these torn and scattered pieces gradually came together until, at Christ's resurrection, they all combined, undoing the damage and revealing the face (see 2 Cor. 3:18; 4:6), the face of God.

The aim of biblical interpretation is to point to the features of this face in the torn pieces of our life and to guide us as to how we should direct our history so that, in it too, the pieces come together, the tears and fragments are knit together, and the face is revealed in all its completeness. "It is God who said, 'Let there be light shining out of darkness,' who has shone in our hearts to radiate the light of the knowledge of God's glory, the glory on the face of Christ" (2 Cor. 4:6).

The interpretation of the Bible is not just neutral knowledge and information. It is and must be an accelerator in the process of remaking life in accordance with the ideal which appeared in the resurrection of Christ. It is an integral part of the process of transformation and liberation of life begun by God when God decided to recover and restore all things in Christ and inaugurate, through him, a new creation.

And when, in the future, the hope is fulfilled, on that day the task of interpretation will be over, because God will be "all in all" (1 Cor. 15:28). Then there will be no more need of interpretation: "There will be no further need for everyone to teach neighbor or brother, saying, 'Learn to know Yahweh!' No, they will all know me, from the least to the greatest" (Jer. 31:34). For now it is as though we are looking into a clouded mirror; then we shall see God as God is (see 1 Cor. 3:12). It is this desire and hope of meeting God again in a totally reconstructed and liberated human life which, in the last analysis, distinguishes the process of Christian interpretation. Through interpretation we try to clean the clouded mirror of life and to contribute to speeding up the process of history, so as to bring about the "new heaven and the new earth" (Rev. 21:1), where the human race will meet God definitively. As long as this future has not arrived, and to make it arrive, the interpreter shouts like the prophet Amos, "Israel, prepare to meet your God" (Am. 4:12).

OLD AND NEW MEET

The Importance of Continuity between Yesterday and Today

Thus far in this chapter I have taken two samples from the river of interpretation, one from the headwaters, from the time of the Fathers of the Church, and the other from the broad curve of the river, from our own time. Then I analyzed the two. The conclusion is already implicit in what I have been saying so far, that is, that there is continuity between yesterday and today—it is the same river! The same vision with which the Fathers read the Bible was present in the eyes of the people when they interpreted the Bible in the João Pessoa meeting.

Some might ask, "Where does this conclusion get us? What use is it?" It is difficult to answer this question because, by the very fact of having asked it, the questioners have shown that they do not see much value in studying the past. But this sort of study does have value.

1. The father's blood is in the child and gives it life, though the child may not realize this. In case of doubt about a child's paternity, a specialist can do a blood test and put the child's mind at rest: "He is your father. Don't listen to gossip! You are legitimate and have the right to inherit!" The people's interpretation, though different and strange, is legitimate. It is an offspring of the church, and has a right to its place. An examination of its genealogy and its blood has proved it. It is a child of the "Fathers," though the people may not realize this. It is a green branch, sprouting from the ancient trunk which was regarded as dead and forgotten, but which has come to life again. Investigation in the church's past has helped to refresh memories, and shows the people's interpretation of the Bible to be legitimate.

2. The study shows too the relativity of the arguments and methods of exegetes and interpreters, be they priests, ministers, or pastoral workers. The continuity of the church's interpretation does not depend on the arguments and methods of the exegetes, but on the church community that in the final analysis is the source of the exegetes' interpretations and purpose. The interpretation coming up from the communities today is the product not so much of the work of interpreters, but more of a re-reading of the Bible carried out by the people in the communities, where faith is mixed with a life of suffering trying to free itself from "captivity."

3. Finally, our study has shown that the people have recovered the correct vision with which Christians should approach the Bible and life. Consequently, despite all its defects and inadequacies, the people's interpretation is a warning sign to exegetes. The exegetes must be at the service of the people's vision, working to foster and clarify it. The people's vision must not be made to fit the view of the exegetes. Rather the exegetes must work to help the people more fully recover their vision of the Bible and life.

The Importance of the Old Testament

"THE NEW TESTAMENT IS CONCEALED IN THE OLD; THE OLD IS REVEALED IN THE NEW"

There is a continuity between creation and salvation. Everything is directed by God to Christ. What is the criterion which enables us to discover this dimension within our history? It is the Old Testament, read and re-read in the light of the New Testament. Therefore, when we analyze, for example, the story of Abraham, we do not do so because of the importance of the Abraham who lived around 1800 B.C., but because of the importance of the Abraham who is today beginning his journey toward Christ.

In one sense, the whole struggle of the people present at the João Pessoa meeting—Indians, farmers, and workers—must be seen as *our* Old Testament. St. Augustine's maxim is true for us too: "The New Testament is concealed in the Old; and the Old is revealed in the New." Or, in other words, Christ and the gospel are present, in a concealed form, in the form of a seed, within the journey and the struggles of our people toward their liberation. On the other hand, this journey should not be analyzed simply and solely in itself, solely as "letter," because it is only revealed and only reveals its full meaning when seen and lived as a journey which will reach its end in Christ.

Without the Old Testament the New Testament cannot be understood, and without the New the Old cannot be understood. The Old Testament is the sounding board which gives resonance and volume to the new words of the gospel. The same is true of us today: the lives of the people, described during the meeting, are for us the backdrop and the resonance chamber which will give us the key to *our* interpretation of the New Testament and of Christ. This history of today is the "letter" within which, with the help of the Bible, we have to discover the "Spirit." Conversely, the people's struggle or journey will go in the right direction and be sure of success only when it lets itself be guided and criticized by its end, which is the resurrection and rebuilding of life in Christ.

THE TENSION BETWEEN THE OLD AND NEW TESTAMENTS

As I said, for the Church Fathers the Old and New Testaments are not simply two consecutive chronological periods. They are also contemporaneous and in tension with each other. From Adam and from Abraham, Christ is already present within history. Everything is already pointing toward him. Christ wants to emerge from our "old" history in order to transform it into a "new" history, but sometimes there is an effort to imprison him in the old history and prevent him from being born.

There are times when the New Testament message is set out explicitly before us. This occurs, for example, in celebrations, masses, the practice of the sacraments, and when the gospel is read; in these situations there is a clear awareness of the presence of Christ. But there are times in which the New Testament slips back below the surface of people's consciousness, and all that is visible is the Old Testament. This occurs when the explicit motivation of faith in Christ is not visible, when what predominates is simply the desire to be free, to survive, not to die of hunger. These struggles for liberation can push Christianity toward Christ; they can also send it into byways which do not lead to resurrection. It is here that we see the service which Christians have to offer oppressed humanity looking for its liberation.

In the time of Jesus some narrow and closed interpretations of the Old Testament tried to force him into paths different from the one which the Father had marked out for him. Jesus always reacted against these "temptations of Satan." He made it clear that the proper criterion for interpreting the word is not interpreting the New in terms of the Old, but interpreting the Old in terms of the New. This still applies today. Our readings of our history, that is, of our Old Testament, may seek to push the church, in the name of science, into a particular path. If this path is not the Father's path, the church will have to react like Jesus, not in the name of another human reading of history, perhaps a conservative one, but in the name of its obedience to the Father. However, when the human reading of history coincides with the Father's project, Jesus does not reject it, but says, "You are not far from the kingdom of God" (Mk. 12:34), or "Whoever is not against me is on my side."

The most disastrous position is that which effects a break

between the Old and New Testaments, between life and faith, between politics and mysticism, between socio-economic liberation and liberation from sin. The tension between the Old and New Testaments is necessary and useful, and has to be accepted and lived consciously by both sides so that, on the one hand, mysticism liberates politics from the limitations and absolutizations inherent in its science, and so that, on the other hand, politics liberates mysticism from the danger of alienation and mystification. The important thing is that all people, whether their positions are aligned more with the "Old" or with the "New," should realize the relativity of their position and should see how much they can receive from the other side. In this area we are still only feeling our way.

IS THE OLD TESTAMENT STILL VALID SINCE THE COMING OF CHRIST?

For all the above reasons I think it is very important to pay more attention to the Old Testament. Keeping just to the New Testament may lead people to miss the profound "political" dimension of Christ's message. The New Testament does not merely sit atop the Old Testament, but rather it grows out of the life and history of the Old Testament and develops it beyond all expectations.

In day-to-day pastoral work the Old Testament is not used much, for a variety of reasons. First, for economic reasons: it is cheaper just to buy the New Testament—the whole Bible costs a lot of money. Second, for reasons of intelligibility: the Old Testament has very difficult passages which people do not understand. Third, for reasons of religious conviction: with the coming of Christ, some people say, the Old Testament was completed and no longer applies to life today.

This last argument is used by some European theologians to criticize the theology of liberation. They say something like this: "We are in the New Testament. The only basis you have for your theology is the Old Testament, but the Old Testament was completed with the coming of Christ. This undermines your whole theological position."

With all due respect to European theologians, I think that this argument is wrong. First, because of our faith in the church.

The church, according to the Council of Trent, accepts and venerates with equal respect, faith, and devotion both the books of the Old Testament and those of the New. If the church accepts both with equal respect, faith, and devotion, we have no right to depreciate one. The second reason comes from everyday experience: Christ has come, but he has not yet come totally in our lives and in our society. He is always coming. No one is completely in the New Testament; no one is 100 percent Christian. Both in Europe and in Latin America, we all have one foot in the Old Testament and one in the New. We are always in transition, trying to renew, to make the old new. Third, we have faith in tradition, which teaches that "grace presupposes nature." The coming of Christ did not cancel what existed before. The Word of God which became flesh did not come to replace the Word which created everything, but to mend and restore the old life which came from Abraham and Adam. A graft cannot grow without a branch to receive it. The fourth reason has to do with the results of scientific investigation: it is not true that the theology of liberation is based only on the Old Testament. We need only to analyze in more detail the meaning of the resurrection, the attitudes of Jesus and especially the book of Revelation, which was written in a period of persecution like our own, to see that what these critics say has little basis. The basis of the theology of liberation is the Old Testament, which is to say, life, but re-read in the light of the New Testament, just as is done in the book of Revelation.

The Service of the Word To Be Performed by the Interpreter

Various things have been said about interpretation:
—It must always start from the "letter," both the "letter" of the past (the text) and the "letter" of the present (the pre-text).
—It should go beyond the "letter" to get to the "Spirit."
—It should use the criteria of science, faith, and solidarity.
—It should go from our Old Testament to the New Testament.
—The Bible cannot be turned into a book of pastoral recipes.
—The process of interpretation has two stages, the return to

the past to discover the text's meaning-in-itself, and the return to the present to discover the meaning-for-us.

— Interpretation is never done in a "neutral" position; it requires the interpreter to take a position.

— In the interpretation of the Bible there must be room for both scientific investigation and the liberating action of the Spirit.

— The Bible has to be read in community, where faith and life are combined in a unity.

— Interpreting is not just teaching and giving information; it is also transforming and bringing to birth.

— We should use the Bible to interpret the book of life.

— We must learn from the "little ones" the right way of looking which enables us to understand the meaning of Jesus' message.

If the interpreter is to achieve all this, what should his or her attitude be? What in practice is this service of the word which the interpreter is meant to offer to the people of God? The first answer might be that interpretation is learned by doing interpretation, but nevertheless there are some rules which can be suggested.

Listening

In their communities the people are beginning to read the Bible as their *own* book. The interpreter, in helping the people in this reading and interpretation, runs the risk of dominating the people with his or her knowledge and so leading them to read the Bible through the eyes of the "expert." If this happens, the interpreter is preventing the people from possessing the word of God as their own.

From this there follows a first task for the interpreter, whether exegete, priest, or pastoral worker. The interpreter must be convinced that, in the interpretation of the Bible, the action of the "Spirit" is as important as the study of the "letter." The interpreter has, and needs to have, the science of the "letter," but does not have, and cannot claim to have, a monopoly on the "Spirit." For the interpreter there must be a time of silence and listening, ear pressed to the ground of life, to understand how the people exercise this new possession of the word of God. This listening is very important if the interpreter is to perform his or her task as interpreter. Knowledge of the "letter" is at the service of the liberating action of the "Spirit," and not the other way round. It is among the people that interpreters must look for the hook on which to hang the results of their study of the "letter." And it is important to remember that the gift of the Spirit operates above all in the communities which contain the "little ones" and where faith exists as part of the people's life of suffering.

TRANSFORMING KNOWLEDGE INTO SERVICE

Popular interpretation is growing strong, full of life and vigor, nourished by oppression and watered by the tears of suffering. On the interpreter's map the roads are nice straight lines running over everything. Only the people who travel along these roads feel their ups and downs, feel the mud, and notice the broken bridges. Only they notice the lack of signposts at crossroads as they wander off into dead ends. On the exegete's map none of these things is marked.

This points to another task for the interpreter. It would be good for the interpreter to come down from the throne of knowledge and ideas and travel along the roads, map in hand, put up signposts, and then use exegetical science, enriched by the traveling, to produce a more detailed and less difficult map, one the people could use, a map corresponding better with the features of the land on which the people walk and suffer.

REMEMBERING WHERE YOU LIVE

Because of the problems which existed in Europe at the end of the last century and the beginning of this one, exegetes had to do an enormous amount of work to defend the historical and literal meaning of the Bible, and piled such a weight of learning on top of the biblical texts that, instead of making access for ordinary people easier, they made it more difficult.

This points to a third task for the interpreter. The interpreter has to realize that the solution to a problem is useful and meaningful only as long as the problem exists. Unfortunately, because of our training, we often carry on giving solutions to problems which have ceased to exist or which are problems in other countries or continents, and as a result we do not see the real problems of the people of God who live in our country or area. As mentioned above, Pope Paul VI in his address to Italian exegetes said that fidelity to the Incarnate Word also demands fidelity to the people of this age who are hearing the message today.

BRINGING TO LIFE THE SITUATION OF THE PEOPLE IN BIBLICAL TIMES

The people, simply following their sense of faith and without any special critical knowledge of the Bible, or of the current situation, run the risk of falling into an alienating, spiritualizing interpretation. If they have a critical awareness only of their own world and not of the biblical text, they may abandon the Bible as a book which is of no help in their struggle.

This gives rise to a fourth task for interpreters. On the one hand they must use all the resources their science can bring to bear on the historico-literal meaning—and these have increased enormously in recent years—to bring to life the situation of the people in biblical times. On the other hand, they must also look deeply into the people's lives in order to find there a "certain connaturality of interests and problems with the subject matter of the text" (Paul VI). In this way the people, who recognize something of themselves and their situation in the Bible, will become better able to see the relevance of their faith to the life they live. Or, as Paul VI put it, "They will be able to open themselves to listen to the text."

USING SCIENCE TO UNDERSTAND TODAY'S WORLD

The interpreter who has a critical awareness of only the biblical text and not of today's world (the pre-text) runs the grave risk of explaining the Bible in accordance with the system that oppresses the people through knowledge, power, and capital. In this case an interpreter, even unwittingly, may keep the Bible on the side of those who teach, order, and pay. And that, with no doubt at all, is not the place where the word of God belongs.

This suggests a fifth task for interpreters. They have to realize that their knowledge is not neutral; they must see that an interpreter cannot remain neutral, because "the person of the interpreter is not detached from the process of interpretation, but is involved in it. The interpreter's whole being is called in question" (Paul VI speaking to the Italian exegetes). So just as, in the first half of this century, science helped interpreters of the Bible to find the courage to expose and denounce the overly dogmatic use of the Bible for the benefit of the established church, in this second half of the century, this same science could help them to find the courage to expose and denounce the overly ideological use of the Bible to benefit established society.

Explaining the Bible in Accordance with the Meaning the Church Gives It

In many places the church is renewing itself and attempting to follow the line of Vatican II and the Medellín documents. However, the people in their daily routine are involved in a difficult conflict with fundamentalists and some Catholics who resist renewal. This gives rise to questions and problems which sharply challenge the church's official line. The point of difference is the Bible, read and re-read with different eyes. It is the conflict between the literal view of the Bible and a view of the Bible linked to life. Surprisingly, in some places Bible study groups turn out to be the groups most resistant to renewal.

This creates a sixth task for interpreters. They have to be imbued with the new vision of the church because, in practice, there is no more effective way of overcoming these conflicts and avoiding these blind alleys than the movement toward liberation to which the church is calling us today. This context of the church as it renews itself by being born of the people offers the best environment for understanding and explaining the meaning of the text of the Bible, a text which can then be used to cast light on the problems raised by the pre-text of today's society.

Explaining the Bible in Accordance with the Church's Ancient Tradition

The simplicity of the gospels enables the people to connect them easily with life. But the Old Testament is a maze. When they get inside, people get lost: they forget how they got in and cannot find the way out. During the basic communities' meeting in João Pessoa, the Indians and some of the workers and peasants, having spent the day thinking about the people's struggle for liberation, spent part of the night in a deep discussion about the story of Adam. At one point a worker said to the Indians: "How can you Indians be descendants of Adam if you were already in Brazil when Cabal came here for the first time?" That question clearly reveals the danger of being trapped within the literal reading of the complex events of the Old Testament.

This gives rise to a seventh task for the interpreter. To answer questions like that, it is not enough to give an explanation of the particular issue raised, because the root of the problem is not a particular issue but the distorted view people have of the Bible. The right view is the one which was always at the root of the Christian interpretation of the Bible and life and which inspired the teaching of the Fathers; it is the view that holds that there is a continuity between creation and salvation. It is impossible to teach a way of looking, but it can be communicated in the process of teaching. If an interpreter has this "right view," we may be quite sure that his or her explanations will gradually help people to discover the path through the Old Testament maze and the exit leading to the New Testament. This view of the Bible and of life works like salt to bring out the full flavor of the language of faith.

CONCLUSION: THE SUFFERING SERVANT OF GOD

Looking at Life with the Bible in Our Eyes

During the basic communities' meeting, while the people were talking about their struggles and sufferings, a very sharp picture kept coming into my mind, the picture of the suffering servant of God whom the prophet Isaiah talks about. In Isaiah's own time the servant was a symbol of the people suffering in captivity, forced into bitter slavery by the power of Nebuchadnezzar.

The story of the suffering servant is told in four songs. In the first song (Is. 42:1–9) God chooses a servant and presents him to the world with the mission of establishing justice on earth (Is. 42:1–4). Then God addresses the servant and calls him to a twofold mission: to unite the people and to be the light of the nations. It is a mission of liberation, because the servant is to open the eyes of the blind and set prisoners free (Is. 42:5–7). God takes responsibility for the servant's mission and guarantees its success (Is. 42:8–9).

In the second song (Is. 49:1–6) Isaiah describes how the servant discovers and accepts his mission, and how he finds inspiration and overcomes the crisis of despair. In the third song the prophet describes how the servant executes his mission: he is persecuted, suffers, but does not turn back. He sets his face like flint because he knows that God, who called him for this mission, will not deceive him (Is. 50:4–9).

Finally, in the fourth song (Is. 52:13–53:12), Isaiah describes the fate of the servant of God as one of suffering. He is a man of sorrows, without charm or beauty, despised by all, with nothing attractive about him, a person people avoid like a leper: "one from whom, as it were, we averted our gaze, despised, for whom we had no regard" (Is. 53:3). He carried the people's sins, and was punished "because of our guilt" (Is. 53:5). "The punishment reconciling us fell on him, and we have been healed by his bruises" (53:5). "Illtreated and afflicted, he never opened his mouth" (53:7). Undefended and denied justice, he was put to death and buried with criminals, he who never committed a crime and never told a single lie (Is. 53:9). For that very reason he will have descendants, will see the light, and will bring justice to all (see Is. 53:10–13).

The prophet Isaiah wrote all this thinking of the people suffering in "captivity," wanting to free themselves but unable to see any escape. The four songs are like four paintings in which the prophet has tried to depict the journey of the suffering people. That is how God would like the people to behave! Jesus looked at these four paintings and guided himself by them in all his life and activity. Because of this he fulfilled the prophecy and became the great suffering servant of God.

Looking at the Bible with Life in Our Eyes

How did Isaiah come to portray the people as a suffering servant? Scholarship tells us that he got the idea from the sufferings of the prophet Jeremiah, who had died a short time before. Jeremiah, despite slander, imprisonment, torture, and persecution, remained faithful to the God of the people of God. His suffering, the fruit of his fidelity, ensured that the people did not lose hope and so contributed to their liberation, though that came much later.

That is why the real meaning of these four songs cannot be discovered simply by studying the vocabulary and the poetry, but needs also and most importantly a reflection on the suffering of Jeremiah as a symbol of the people's suffering. This applies today as well. It is not enough to study the "letter" of the four songs. It is also necessary to see the people who, like Jeremiah, symbolize the suffering of the people. They can reveal the full meaning of the text because they live what Isaiah attempted to describe.

During the meeting in João Pessoa one person in particular revealed for me the meaning of this mysterious prophecy about the suffering servant as the image of the whole people suffering. She was from Maranhão. A friend pointed her out to me and said, "She is the living image of the suffering servant of God." And she was.

The people from Maranhão arrived at the meeting late. We were already in the lobby after supper, chatting, when someone said, "Here comes Maranhão!" I looked and saw a group of people coming up the steps. In front came a woman who walked with some difficulty, limping, almost swaying. She was leading by the hand a blind man with black trousers and straw-colored hair; he was carrying an old accordion on his back. The two poor people were welcomed with lots of hugs. There is nowhere else where they would have been invited to represent their people in any assembly. The people to go would be the most important, the best looking.

This woman was from the diocese of Viana. Because of political changes that had taken place there she was asked to leave the diocese. She left and went to another diocese, where she continued with the same work. ("Have you been questioned by the police?" "Yes, thank God!") Apparently ignorant, still suffering the effects of childhood polio, she is very disfigured, her head, arms and legs all twisted; she has no physical beauty. But there is nothing wrong with her mind, and happiness shines from her eyes. She ponders and reasons like no one else, and knows what she wants. In the review session at the end of the meeting she picked on two negative aspects. First, "We came here to represent not just our towns, but the states as well. But lots of people forgot to mention the rest of the state and kept to their own little town." Second, "One thing I thought was wrong was that people didn't help with the cooking and cleaning. I saw that there was a need and grabbed a brush or a cloth and set to work." In other words, she was a woman with a concern to see the whole picture and was also able to notice the little gaps in practical arrangements.

She is a living commentary on Isaiah's four songs of the servant. There are scholarly commentaries by learned exegetes, the result of lengthy study, which show us how Isaiah came to write his prophecy. Dona Maria is also the result of lengthy studies, carried out by learned people working for the system and produced to find better ways of dominating and exploiting the people. She is also the result of lengthy suffering, of centuries of oppression of a whole people, of the weak by the powerful, by landowners, by the owners of machinery, by the system, by the church.

The Life Which Illuminates the Bible Is Illuminated by the Bible

To understand the meaning of the texts of the prophet Isaiah about the suffering servant we need the written commentaries of scholars, but they are not enough. We also need the living commentary, as lived by the people who suffer, a commentary visible in the life of Dona Maria and in the lives of many others like her all over the world. The Bible and the suffering lives of the people are like mirrors which catch the light of God and cast it back and forth between them. In this process the light increasingly illuminates the Bible and the people's lives. There is a mutual influence of life on the Bible, and of the Bible on life. One without the other can only be half seen and understood. So what is the light which the suffering lives of people like Dona Maria and the others assembled in João Pessoa receive from Isaiah's prophecy of the suffering servant?

Like the suffering servant described by Isaiah, these people too are called by God to a great mission, and are introduced into the world by God to establish law and justice on earth. Like that other servant, today as well the suffering people undergo crises in their faith, thinking that their lives and work are worthless. But the moment they discover the mission God has given them, there is no power in the world which can defeat them. In that moment they are liberated inwardly and begin to see the power which oppresses them. In their own way, they begin to resist. Docile like the servant, they listen to what God has to say to them (see Is. 49:1) and do not flinch. They set their faces like flint, because they have faith in the God who supports and sends them. Like the servant, they are despised, humiliated, and marginalized. They suffer the pains of all humanity. Deformed and without physical beauty, they are avoided like lepers. But they go on, even if it costs them their lives, just like Jesus, who, by his life, death, and resurrection, teaches the people how to fulfil the prophecy about God's suffering servant.

3

Defenseless Flower:
The People's Reading
of the Gospel
in the Context of Life

Flower, you turn blood into fertilizer!
You are stronger than the hand which cuts you,
More enduring than the idea which defines you,
Brighter than the paint which portrays your face.
The world is growing afraid of you,
Defenseless flower!

INTRODUCTION TO THE PROBLEM

"Sister, I'm not going to say anything because I don't understand these things. I'm just going to listen and learn." That was Dona Getulina's reply when Sister Vicentina asked her if she could give an opinion on the Bible passage read in the meeting. Another woman, Dona Florentina, did not give the Sister time to reply, but cut in: "Dona Getulina, you mustn't say you don't know anything. You have the Holy Spirit. He speaks to you and you pass on his message to us."

Getulina and Florentina live in a poor district of a town in Minas Gerais, Brazil. They have no course credits or degrees.

55

When asked about their profession, they reply "mother" or "housewife." Ordinary women.

When people like this get hold of the Bible, a strange phenomenon occurs; it is almost automatic. Either they go through a rebirth and become free in relation to other people's knowledge and power, or they are trapped and become dependent on that knowledge and power.

Where people are reborn, one realizes the truth of St. Paul's remark: "Where the Spirit of the Lord is, there is freedom" (2 Cor. 3:17). But where the people become weak and get tangled up in the details of the Bible, one draws another conclusion which Paul drew: "Their hearts are covered with a veil" (2 Cor. 3:13, 15), and so they do not see the point of their lives and history.

The Bible either helps or hinders, either liberates or oppresses. It is not neutral. It is like a double-edged knife: it always cuts, for better or worse. It exercises a form of judgment; it "can seek out the place where soul is divided from spirit, or joints from marrow; it can pass judgment on secret emotions and thoughts" (see Heb. 4:12). It reveals the quality of the light inside us.

How is the Bible contributing in practice to the liberation of the people? This is the question I found myself asking as I read a series of reports on the base communities. The answer I found as I read on was that the biblical text alone, or study of the text, is not enough to ensure the Bible will act as a contributor to liberation. The text is the same for everyone. What is not the same is its effect, and the obvious conclusion one can reach from that is that factors external to the text have much to do with whether the Bible functions as a liberative force in the people's lives.

Further consideration of the above question and conclusion led me to realize this: where the reading and explanation of the biblical text are done within a proper *context* and on the basis of a proper *pre-text,* then a flower grows. It is a small, fragile flower, which brings into question all the knowledge we have hitherto acquired about flowers.

This strange, weak flower does not fit the criteria of our logic and demands their reformulation. It makes an appeal to logic and says, "Recognize that I am a different sort of flower. Change your way of thinking about flowers and come and help me so that I can grow and come into full bloom. Only in this way will you be able to enjoy the beauty of my colors and the fragrance of my scent."

THE REPORTS ON WHICH THESE REFLECTIONS ARE BASED

The reports were prepared from a questionnaire which had groups of questions on five different topics. (It would be good to mention here that except where otherwise noted, quotations in this chapter are from these reports.) There was a total of thirty-eight questions. I noticed that among the thirty-eight questions there was not one on the use of the Bible. I thought this was excellent. Since there was no specific question, the answer would be diffused through the other answers, and if the Bible was really contributing to the liberation of the people, this would appear automatically. And it did. The Bible was referred to more in some reports than in others, but it was at least mentioned in every report except one.

Since my task was not so much to interpret what the reports said as to get through to the situations they described, I took the liberty of fleshing out the skeleton of reports with facts I experienced myself or learned from others. This gave more detail and background.

When one is dealing with a "church born from the people," there are only two experts: the Holy Spirit and the people themselves, who always work in close cooperation and communicate by means we are unaware of. The role of the other "experts" is, as suggested in one of the reports, "to exchange ideas so as to discover the Holy Spirit's idea among the people." The "experts" are invited to become students of the current practice of the church, which confirms the truth of Jesus' saying: "I bless you, Father, Lord of heaven and earth, for hiding these things from the learned and the clever and revealing them to these little ones. Yes, Father, for that is what it pleased you to do" (Mt. 11:25–26).

Working from this understanding of the role of "experts," I shall try in this chapter to do the following: reflect on what is going on and see how the Bible is really being used by the people, how it is contributing to the formation of basic ecclesial communities, how it is inserted into education for liberation, how it is making the people more aware. I shall try to discover if this use of the Bible at the base is in accord with what faith teaches about the use of the Bible, try to discover what theory emerges from this practice, and try to see if the representatives of scholarship (exegetes) and of the faith (clergy) are carrying out their mission. Finally, I want to see how the theory which emerges from the practice can provide better guidance both for the work of interpreters, priests, and pastoral workers and for the attitude of the people themselves toward the Bible, so that the Bible might make a better contribution to attaining its objective, "that the people may have life, and have it in abundance" (see Jn. 10:10).

THE PRESENT STATE OF THE MATTER: WHERE, WHEN, AND HOW THE PEOPLE USE THE BIBLE

Something new is happening. The people feel a great love for the word of God; there is a familiarity with the Psalms and biblical texts.

They meet to reflect on the gospel in the context of the problems of their own lives, and on the causes and consequences of those problems.

At first sight, so our education tells us, the problem of the use of the Bible in the church has to do with the transmission of items of information about the meaning of the text in itself.

This way of looking at the interpretation of the word of God, while not wrong, is incomplete. When someone, relying on this view alone, begins to push the cart of pastoral action, he or she will go off into byways or maybe never get moving at all.

Knowledge of the text is only one wheel of the vehicle of interpretation. If the other wheels are not working well, however good the wheel of textual knowledge may be, the vehicle will not move forward.

The people are beginning to move the other wheels, and

the vehicle has already started moving, slowly for the moment, but it has begun to move. In the following sections I shall try to give a portrait of how the people are doing this. I shall try to offer a glimpse of where, when, and how the people use the Bible.

Discussion Groups

The increase in the number of groups in which ordinary people are beginning to "read the gospel in life" is the most striking phenomenon in the current renewal of the church. All the reports talk about this, though it is difficult to carry out a detailed survey of everything being done in this area. The general picture is summed up in this remark by a man from one of the communities: "Now, since we've started learning to read the Bible, we're finding things from real life in it."

There is no fixed model for these discussion groups. There is just a very simple, common, basic pattern — a fact or real-life situation compared with a Bible reading, with some questions to start general discussion. Around this basic pattern there may be all sorts of variations, some more complicated and sophisticated, others simpler, some more searching, others more superficial.

Sometimes the real-life incident is chosen in advance by a team and put to the people at the meeting. At other times it is taken directly from the experiences of those who make up the group: each person mentions the most important thing that happened to him or her in the past week. The biblical text may also be chosen in advance by a team or chosen in response to the issues raised by the group. This second approach obviously demands considerable familiarity with the Bible.

Sometimes the meeting is every two weeks, sometimes once a week. In some places the cycle is not fixed. The meeting is held when there is a widespread problem, and groups have been known to meet then as often as twice or three times a week.

The groups come into being for a great variety of reasons: a Christmas novena in people's houses, the national lenten campaign, preparation for Holy Week, the need to address problems that affect many, and so on. Or it may be the result of a gradual process: "The work started with the teachers, the rosary leaders, the catechists, backed by the priest. They felt that just praying wasn't solving the people's problems. So the idea emerged of reading the gospel in life."

The whole phenomenon of the people reading the Bible in the communities can be compared to a long road. From the beginning to the end there are people on the move, all going more or less in the same direction, though some are temporarily on byways or dead ends; here and there certain persons are trying to help the people stay on course; some of the people are already very near the end, others just at the beginning. The means of transport used to get to the end of the road have various names, "discussion groups," "Bible circles," "family circles," "house celebrations," "Bible groups," "group meetings," "Bible meetings," "movements," or just "meetings." The label is of little importance. The important thing is that everyone is trying to do more or less the same thing, "to read the gospel in the context of life" or "exchange ideas so as to discover the Holy Spirit's idea among the people."

To give something of the flavor of what goes on in these groups, here is one woman's account of a meeting; the account was given in the midst of an informal conversation:

Lots of people are full of tradition, stuck. We used to be like that. But now, with these Bible and community meetings, we're beginning to realize that we're people. Many people don't realize what this means. There's so much injustice, and even more fear, even in the community. What really paralyzes you is fear. One person on her own can't cope and is afraid. These meetings are good because they help us to discover that we were made to be free. That's why I like, I've always liked, life in the church. I pray a lot—you should see me! As often as I can. The other day a man called Zé Maria came into the meeting; he means very well, but he's very wrapped up in the Bible—he overdoes it! He was talking a lot and kept quoting chapter and verse at people, putting them down. Almost like the sects. It really got on your nerves. So I took my time with him. You have to take your time and be able to wait. So I said, "Zé Maria, does your wife understand you? Do your daughters understand you when you talk like that?" He said they didn't. I said, "You see! People have to understand, Zé Maria, or what's the point?" Now he's begun to change a little. He's beginning to understand. He's beginning to see how you do things.

At the root of this phenomenon of the spread of groups seems to be the desire to "form a community church, in which people can take on tasks and take responsibility for themselves, with the values they have discovered in themselves"; the groups are also fostered by the desire of the people to escape from the massification and anonymity which threaten everyone today with oppression and alienation; finally, the groups flower because they enable the people to find in their unity the strength which will enable them to overcome the power which oppresses and crushes their lives. As one woman said: "This work is creating more unity here and elsewhere. Now people see that it's possible to do something. I've lost my fear." Through the establishment of small groups, in which everyone has a right to speak, people are beginning to discover their own worth: "The good thing about this movement of ours is that we feel we're people with other people to support us."

Bible Circles

Strictly speaking, any group attempting to "read the gospel in the context of life" could be called a "Bible circle." In reality, it seems that the term is used only for those groups which usually follow a fixed program prepared by others.

In the past there used to be Bible circles whose main purpose was to help the people to acquire greater knowledge of the content of the Bible. Today the aim is different: to get people to look at their lives in the light of the gospel and with its perspective, and as far as possible channel everyone into community activity. In some places the spread of Bible circles is the first sign of renewal. They are stimulated by the priest or spread on their own "with the aim of making the people move from being hearers of the word to proclaimers of it."

In communities with more experience this form of biblical meeting tends to decrease and be replaced by a less structured and less directed form. These are known as "house celebrations," which are less intellectual and involve the participants more.

This transition from more structured Bible circles to a less structured and more involving type of meeting shows that the Bible circles are not an end in themselves. They are scaffolding, only used while the building is being built. They are a stage in a journey: they take the traveler only to an intermediate station. Anyone who wants to get to the end of the journey has to take another form of transport. Bible circles with programs prepared by outsiders produce their fruit and show that they are working effectively when they set off a process which makes them unnecessary.

In addition, it is important to remember that Bible circles usually start from the analysis of a real-life incident. As the groups make progress in analyzing individual incidents, they realize that the incidents are the product of a general situation, and that therefore it is necessary to go further than analyzing particular incidents.

The simpler and less complicated the structure of a Bible circle, the faster it leads to the intermediate station, to the critical point where the travelers must change to another form of transport. But whatever happens, even if the more or less rigid system of Bible circles is abandoned, the basic attitude remains the same, from beginning to end: "reading the gospel in the context of life."

Celebrations of the Word

In many places the clergy have promoted or are promoting a degree of decentralization of worship, allowing the people to be more creative, more active, and more autonomous in expressing their faith. On all sides what are called "celebrations of the word" are springing up in which the people celebrate their liturgy, and read and explain the word of God, without the presence of a priest. The name varies: "celebration of the word," "liturgical prayer," "house celebrations," "Sunday liturgy," and so on. The conviction which inspired this decentralization is this: "We believe that the word of God expressed by the people really succeeds in translating the gospel into ordinary·life."

Generally the people use prepared leaflets which give readings and prayers. Some are beginning to feel free enough to change the readings: "When a problem arises in the community, we choose a reading which is right for the celebration. It's been producing results. There's already a change—less gossip, more friendship." "Take the celebrations, for example. We meet and prepare them on the basis of what's happening in the town. It comes straight from us."

The commentaries on the readings, in most cases, are done by everyone present. They take various forms: reflection combined with discussion and exchange of ideas, dramatizations with audience reaction, meditative commentaries in the form of a prayer without discussion, singing and music, and so on.

The place where the celebrations take place varies according to custom and possibilities. It may be the village chapel, if there is one, families' houses, any shed or larger building, or it may be under the shade of a tree. In general, in most of the areas that reported there does not seem to be much difference between the number of people who attend Masses and the number of those attending the celebrations of the word without a priest.

This greater participation and relative autonomy of the people in the liturgy have been, and for many people still are, the beginning of renewal and the way to a new sense of the church. "The worship sector is the starting point of all the community activity which develops and strengthens the people's unity." "All the other activities have grown out of this celebration of the word, which we regard as the great source of strength."

Not everything is positive. As we shall see, there is the danger of a covert control by the clergy in these celebrations, when the leader of the liturgy imitates the role of the priest and monopolizes everything, without giving the people present the opportunity to speak and give their opinion.

Courses and Training Programs

On every side, where the church is undergoing renewal, courses, training programs, and meetings are springing up. And there is not a training session, a meeting, or a course in which the Bible is not used in some way or other. This can be seen from the programs of these events, which were described in some reports.

These courses have awakened many minds and have given rise to many new and original vocations. Antônio dos Anjos, sixty-eight years old, a rubber-tapper from Alto Acre, said:

> The instructors' course did me a lot of good. I always intended to follow God's teaching. I thanked God for that time in October 1973 when I met the Sisters and the priest in Assis, Brazil, who invited me. I was living in quite a lot of darkness, but now I have more light. I am protected by God and call everyone brother and sister.

Antônio now goes around on foot, visiting the inhabitants of the rubber-tapper settlements, covering more than sixty miles a month. "On these visits I announce the word of God to everyone," he says.

Both at the start of Antônio's individual conversion and at the start of a number of communities, we find a course which awakened the group for the search for liberation. For example, a course on the "history of salvation" helped to start the process for a community in the parish of Poranga.

These courses, meetings, and training programs also respond to the need felt by the people for a deeper understanding of their faith and a more solid formation. As a result, afternoon Bible courses are organized, particularly for instructors. However, as we shall see, the institutionalization of permanent courses may have the opposite effect to the one intended, and keep people feeling dependent on someone else's knowledge.

As the process of renewal takes shape and becomes established, the form and content of the courses change. "More than courses, they become reflection on action and on the work done with the people."

Mass

Participation by the people in the use of the Bible is also increasing in official liturgical celebrations, presided over by the clergy: (1) Masses in which the first part, called "the liturgy of the word," is organized by representatives of the people present; (2) Masses with dialogue sermons, in which the people take an active part in the commentary on the gospel; (3) Masses in which the first reading becomes an account of a significant incident in the community (once the reader even began, "A reading from the acts of the Christians of Agua Rasa"); (4) Masses in which the reading of the gospel is replaced by a dramatic representation of the gospel.

Despite all this increase in participation by the people in the official liturgy, it is important to remember the great difference which exists between "the official celebration of the liturgy, in which the people are customers, and the ritual expressions of their own worship, where they are the initiators." It is also important to remember this statement: "A nervous, stumbling reading done by a member of the community has more of the flavor of liberation than a polished and educated reading by a priest or Sister."

"At Mass there is a debate in which all have an opportunity to speak and say what they think. Only a few years ago we used to go to services only in Lent and Holy Week. Now we do the preparation, and when the priest arrives we've already done it. The group meets, along with other people, and we try to see what issue or problem is uppermost in people's minds, and we look in the gospel to see which passage is most relevant to this issue or problem."

In a community in a remote area of Ceará state, around thirty people were gathered in the little mud chapel. It was night, the feast of Candlemas. The Bible text, read by the light of a single oil lamp, spoke of the aged Simeon recognizing Christ as the light of the world, a light apparently as weak as the light of the oil lamp, since it came hidden in the form of a poor baby, brought to the Temple by a poor couple. Then six other lamps or candles were lit and filled the little chapel with light, without lessening the light of the first lamp. The question was asked: "Which of you has discovered God's hidden light in the life you live?" João, the union secretary, replied: "I have. It was the day before yesterday. One candle lit another six, when a man asked six other men from the community to go and help Zé, who's battling on his own against the landowner. The owner wants to throw him off the land, and has already given orders to pull up the cotton Zé's planted."

Theater, Art, and Music

There is a variety of attempts to use the Bible to give recognition to the people's artistic talents.

THEATER

Some reports speak of dramatizations without giving details. On occasion there are references to biblical plays. I have seen or read plays created by the people for Christmas, Easter, and other events in the Christian calendar. Usually drama is part of courses and training programs. When used to give people a better understanding of the Bible, drama produces excellent results. It is more intuitive, is more able to get through to the heart and to real life; it stimulates involvement and encourages creativity. Drama can be used in various ways. A biblical scene can be presented literally, or there can be a modernized version of the biblical story in which the Bible and ordinary contemporary life are shown as more united. Another way is a dramatization of some incident of contemporary life with a commentary at the end in the form of a reading of a biblical text.

MUSIC

Once I saw someone give a commentary on the Bible with songs accompanied by a violin. For more than an hour they sang popular Brazilian songs, interweaving phrases and stories from the Bible. It was a strikingly original performance, and the singer covered the stories of the exodus, the prophets, and Jesus' journeys around Palestine, and Paul's travels to the first Christian communities. And all the commentary came from well-known Brazilian songs, giving familiar words and music a new context and new connotations. In many places, for instance in the Northeast of Brazil, the gospel text is the inspiration for new liturgical songs.

OTHER ART FORMS

I have seen and heard traveling singers in the Northeast sing the story of Abraham. There are cheap comic books "which talk of Amos, a prophet and peasant like us." St. Matthew's gospel has been produced in comic book form. Various reports mention poems and songs produced within the communities. There is a modern, rhyming version of a gospel parable; the version is called "The Appetizer." Here and there the people are beginning to attempt to represent biblical scenes and characters in paintings and sculpture. One diocese has a special pastoral program to foster people's art: "The people's art and values form a well of riches in which the 'seeds of the word' are concentrated. Evangelization should try to discover and develop these assets."

Popular Religious Practices

The Bible is being used in a number of ways in the communities to renew traditional expressions of popular religion. Here are some examples from the reports:

1. Gospel readings with reflections on life were introduced into the novenas.

2. One community worked out a plan to "celebrate the St. John's day bonfire by getting all the districts together in one place, celebrating the word of God, and then having fun."

3. "There was an attempt to renew the tradition of the Epiphany follies, giving a more gospel-based and communal flavor to the words of the songs."

4. "Last Christmas, when there was an elaborate production in popular style, liberation, in the context of an analysis of the situation, was the dominant theme of the 'follies,' plays,

poems, songs, and other events. It made a vast and eloquent statement."

Sometimes the following process takes place. Once people have started to take part in the meetings and "family circles" to "reflect on the Bible and everyday problems, they start to like them and prefer these meetings to novenas and more traditional practices." The people get to a stage where they appeal to the authority of the gospel and resist "the sacramental pattern in which the hierarchical monopoly still predominates in day-to-day decisions."

Private Reading

Only two reports explicitly mention private Bible reading. This is understandable, since there was no question about this. Nevertheless the custom of reading the Bible at home, alone or as a family, is widespread. I know simple people with little education who know the Bible almost by heart. The bulletin *Nós Irmaos* (*We are Brothers and Sisters*) from Acre encourages daily Bible reading, giving a list of texts, one for each day of the month.

Methods of private reading vary enormously. I heard the following two accounts during conversations with two people from the communities; they give us a glimpse of the various ways people read the Bible privately in the midst of their day-to-day lives.

Altamiro, owner of a little store in a remote part of Minas Gerais, gave this account: "I have so much faith in the Bible, in the word of God, that I open it with my eyes closed at any page. And I tell you, so far I've always found a message. It's never failed. God doesn't fail."

Neusa is a cleaner and mother of six children. She lives in a favela in Belo Horizonte. One day she asked me, "What does it mean when it says, 'It's a terrible thing to fall into the hands of the living God'? I read that sentence in the Bible last night. I've asked several people, but none of them could tell me. Every night I read a bit of the Bible, one or two chapters—it depends." "Do you read it in sequence, or how do you read it?" I asked. "No," she replied. "I read from where I open it. Sometimes it's chapter 5, sometimes it's chapter 10 or 30. As it happens. But yesterday I read three chapters in a row—I don't know why—and there was that sentence. I felt sort of dizzy. But I hadn't had anything to eat, so I left it. They say that ignorant people shouldn't read the Bible; it only causes confusion. But I like reading the Bible, at night, at home, when I get in from work. I like the things of God, you know. I don't bother with all the other nonsense. I think it's a waste of time."

CRITIQUING THE PEOPLE'S USE OF THE BIBLE

Very rarely, almost always by accident, one manages to get through to what goes on inside people's lives. When this happened to me as I read the reports, I was very surprised to find how many very old customs continued, even in people who are most active in the renewal. We may shake our heads and smile at some of the attitudes of the "ignorant" people. We may even label them "naive." But a smile does not change the reality, and a label does not alter the content. And which of us has the authority to say that the content is worthless?

All of the information discussed thus far in this chapter shows how and when the people use the Bible. It gives us a cross section of the continuing practice of the people as regards the Bible. Not everything is new. Much has always been there. It is just that we are only now directing our eyes and our attention toward it to discover and analyze it. This reality exists independently of the fact that we are for or against it. And, to tell the truth, it exists a little in each of us. In it everything is mixed up and grows together, the tares and the wheat, the strengths and the weaknesses.

Only a person who has studied and is doing research tries to distinguish between the strengths and the weaknesses. Most people do not usually make the distinction. For them everything seems to be valuable because they nourish everything with the sap of their lives, their faith and their common sense, both the tares and the wheat. It remains to be seen if the "expert," who tries to separate the tares from the wheat, the weaknesses from the strengths, uses the right criteria. After all, it is well known that people from rural areas live very well on plants which, for townspeople, are no more than scrub and weeds. That is why it is dangerous for the "expert" to launch into "weeding," separating the tares from the wheat, before the time is right.

Aware of this limitation, I shall try to give an opinion, though I know that it must be provisional. The factors I shall use as a basis for shaping my opinion are these: the statements contained in the reports, the fruits borne by each type of use of the Bible (since it is by the fruits that we know the tree), and my study of the history of the use of the Bible in the church. The way I shall frame the "critique" is as follows: I shall set out the character-istics and the strengths of popular interpretation, describe its difficulties and weaknesses, and, finally, make some observations on the method used by the people in interpreting the Bible. Basing my analysis on this critique of the people's use of the Bible, I shall then move on, in subsequent sections of this chap-ter, to address the central problem of biblical interpretation, the repercussions of popular exegesis, and the issue of how to build a genuinely liberative education.

Strengths of the People's Use of the Bible

To exchange ideas so as to discover the Holy Spirit's idea among the people.

This renewal in the church is dangerous because it brings responsibility with it.

A MIRROR OF LIFE

In the people's eyes the Bible and life are connected. When they open the Bible they want to find in it things directly related to their lives, and in their lives they want to find events and meanings that parallel those in the Bible. Spontaneously they use the Bible as an image, symbol, or mirror of what is happen-ing to them here and now. Sometimes they even confuse the two and say, "Our Bible is our life."

They do not always succeed in making a firm connection be-tween the Bible and their lives. Sometimes they make arbitrary connections, with no basis in the text of the Bible or in the reality of life today. But that does not diminish or invalidate the profound intuition present in everything the people do with the Bible: the Bible has to do with life. It takes a period of learning before people get to the point where they can say, "Since we have learned to read the Bible, we've been finding the stuff of our lives in it."

Antônio, a man from the hinterlands of Ceará, after hearing an explanation of the story of Abraham, said, "Now I understand: we're like Abraham. We travel like him, without being sure where the journey will lead. Outside everything is uncertain, but inside we have a certainty: this is what God wants of us. If Abraham succeeded, we too will be able to succeed. We must just keep on and not lose heart." For Antônio the story of Abraham is not just a story from the past; it has also become a mirror which reflects the story of his own life back to him. He will go on reading this story, not only to learn what happened to other people, but also in order to learn what God wants to achieve in him. In the Bible he finds something of himself and his aspirations.

This view of the Bible as a critical reflection of our world awakens people and makes them seekers. The Bible is read and studied in order to know better the present situation and the calls from God that exist in it. The ultimate aim of the people's use of the Bible is *not so much to interpret the Bible, but to interpret their lives.* "The gospel has been compared to a mirror. It's true: Our lives are reflected in the gospel, and the gospel is reflected back into our lives. Our first and foremost use of the gospel is to compare it with our world in order to get a better idea of the shape of our lives. Once you've discovered the gospel, life joins in a duet with it, harmonizing even in the most trivial details." The Bible helps people to understand the world, and the world helps them to understand better the meaning of the Bible. The two cannot be separated.

At a diocesan meeting held in a rural area of Ceará, the epistle of the Mass was replaced by the following reading:

A reading from the acts of the Christians of Agua Rasa.
At that time, Antônio and Esmeralda, an old couple, mar-

ried for over fifty years, passed by the house where the Christians were meeting. Alfredo, one of the Christians, invited them in. They were reluctant: "We're following the animals, and we've only six more miles to go." Alfredo insisted, and they stopped. They went in and were introduced to the others. It was the first time that anyone had taken an interest in the lives and work of the two old people. At one point a woman asked, "Antônio and Esmeralda, tell me one thing. In your married life have you always been happy?" The old couple did not say anything; the reply was two blissful smiles as they hugged each other, as if to say "What a question!" Alfredo spoke to the others: "See the great hidden thing which God has been doing among us for almost fifty years and which God has only now revealed to us." Here ends the reading from the acts of the Christians of Agua Rasa.

The Bible was not mentioned; its place was taken by life. Alfredo reads the Bible every day for fifteen to twenty minutes. The result of this constant ruminating on the word of God is the purity of vision which is able to discover and reveal to others the signs of the presence of God in the simplest aspects of the people's life.

This intimate connection between the Bible and life is revealed also in the ease with which the people in the communities use biblical themes and characters to describe present-day situations: the oppression the people endure and their work for liberation are like the captivity in and exodus from Egypt; the communities' struggles with landowners are likened to David's battle with Goliath; the people's long but hopeful struggle, laden with suffering and temporary defeats, is compared with Jesus' suffering, death, and resurrection.

All this recalls St. Paul saying that the story of Abraham is a symbol (Heb. 11:19). It also recalls a statement by Origen that summarizes the Fathers' attitude toward the Bible: "What we look for in the Bible is not just the history but also the symbol, the allegory."

"OUR BOOK, WRITTEN FOR US"
In a rural area of the state of Minas Gerais, a landowner on whose land the community chapel was built refused to take the

course the community required for parents and godparents. He got angry and threatened to close the chapel. The coordinator, a very simple peasant, replied calmly, "You can close the chapel, but you can't catch or tie down the word of God." The landowner may own the land, but he does not own the word of God. That belongs to the people, and the people are beginning to acquire the sense of freedom which that word gives to those who make it their own.

The people regard themselves as those to whom the Bible is directly addressed. They receive it from God and the church (and not from the priest or the exegete) as *their* book. They firmly believe that God speaks directly to them through the Bible. They do not read it furtively, as though they were reading a letter addressed to someone else. On the contrary, they continue to repeat St. Paul's saying, "This was written for us!" (1 Cor. 10:11). They feel the word of God as an immediate presence and translate its meaning into the here and now.

This is the source of their gratitude, respect, and inner freedom in relation to the Bible. And it is true that the people use the Bible with enormous respect, great freedom, and immense gratitude. They live the gratuitousness of the word of God, which, very often, apart from their children, is the only wealth they have in their poverty.

In a refresher course for community coordinators, the following question was asked: "In your view, what most helps people to grow?" The reply came immediately: "The word of God!" One of them, returning home at night after instructing the parents and godparents, said, "I said a few poor words to them. If they didn't like it, it's not my fault; I took them from the Lord's book!"

"Something new is happening. The people feel a great love for the word of God; there is a familiarity with the Psalms and the biblical texts." In one of the reports there is talk of the "reappropriation of the Bible by the people." And lay people keep saying, "The Bible has become accessible to us. It's been given to the laity. We feel at home with it."

The phrase "at home" sums up the situation: the Bible has become familiar, part of the family, "our Bible." The people "read the Bible in the liturgy and outside it. From it they draw stories of God's action, principles of deep wisdom, the mysteries of Christ, and his vision of the kingdom. They discuss these treasures together, relating them to their everyday lives, and in the process the first revolution takes place, one which is fundamental, Pentecostal: each person moves from a knowledge received to a knowledge discovered."

Gradually, shared reading of and reflection on the word of God create a family atmosphere: "Everyone knows everyone else, and they all display their pleasure at the meetings; they're ready to help each other." The word is gathering together and creating a community, and the community in its turn offers the environment, the *context,* for the reading of the word. Someone defined the basic ecclesial communities as "the people gathering to look for Christ's word."

The shared reading gives rise to shared activities, as problems are faced. The shared activities give rise to a new sense of mission in the world, of being at the service of the human community.

This sense of community, nourished by the conviction expressed in the slogan, "Our book, written by God for us," is growing in the various meetings, communities, and celebrations. It is like a very fine net, invisible at first, whose filaments are being woven together in the secrecy of individual choices made in contact with the word, with other people, and with society.

This is how the church is born, the *ecclesia* in the strictest and most literal sense of the term, *the group called together by the word for a mission.* This church is the *context* in which the people read the *text* of the Bible. Without this context, the text would be like a light disconnected from the power.

This new community sense is also reflected in the way the people have begun to pay more attention to their own history: "Each community has its history and builds its history." This reflection on their own history and situation creates the space required for the word of God to be received.

WITH THE LIGHT OF FAITH IN THEIR EYES

St. Paul wrote to the Corinthians that the letter kills, but the Spirit gives life. The light of faith which is in our eyes lights up the letter and gives it life. This was happening in St. Paul's day, and is happening in our own as well.

At root, the people's faith in the Bible is not faith in a book, but faith in Someone speaking today through the book. What gives meaning and life to the book is this faith in the living Christ present in life and in the community. The people's remarks, as recorded in the reports from the communities, leave no doubt about this: "The person of Christ is a real presence and a dynamic force in everything." "I've begun to treat people with much more respect than before. I have met the living Christ among us, the Christ who lives hidden and silent among us. Previously God was a distant being; now God walks alongside us, and Jesus is our brother."

Other reports speak of the presence and action of the Holy Spirit: "You can feel the power of the Holy Spirit." There is a deep trust "in the active presence of the Holy Spirit within the people." Instead of contemplating and "writing lives of the saints, of individuals, the time has come to write the lives of communities: we will discover a richer, deeper, and more fruitful presence of the Holy Spirit among us." "There is a great sensitivity among the people to the 'signs' which appear in attitudes, gestures, and events, as hints of the presence and action of the Spirit." We have "to exchange ideas so as to discover the Holy Spirit's idea among the people."

I could go on like this, quoting sayings which show flashes of the light in the people's eyes. This is the light by which they read the Bible, choosing and selecting texts in relation to problems which arise.

This light *must not go out* because, if it goes out, the text of the Bible will be left in darkness and the written word will be powerless. Hence the need constantly to devote energy to keeping this light burning. This explains why the Bible must be read above all in an environment of prayer. Prayer intensifies this light, and that is why there is an increasing desire among the communities for a stronger prayer life. Prayer gives the Holy Spirit a chance to enlighten minds and reveal where God is speaking today through the world and society.

This light is not the privilege of a few "experts" or intellectuals. It is the gift of God, given to the community and, through the community, to the individuals who make it up. Hence the need for the community context for Bible reading. Even individual reading is not, and cannot be, a purely private matter. Reading the Bible alone or in community strengthens and nourishes one's commitment to God and others, and increases the desire for freedom for individuals and the community.

A strong tree on which an axe makes no mark will fall in the wind if the roots rot. Freedom is a strong young tree growing ever stronger. Its roots grow and do not rot, but spread through the soil of the life of the oppressed people when those people, in the ordinary trivial affairs of every day, are able to be in the company of Someone who is really free. God is free and brings freedom. This has been the characteristic of God's name since the beginning. Contact with this God nourishes in the people the desire to cultivate and foster their freedom, and guides that desire so that it does not go astray.

Once a priest dedicated to promoting "the experience of the living God" among the people said, "I'm uncertain. Is this a genuine experience, or is it just a new wrapping to protect an old form of religion unconnected with real life?" I replied, "Look at the results and analyze them. If you can't find there any work for liberation, any struggle for justice, any attempt to analyze society, if life is not becoming more human, then it is probable that the people are coming into contact with an idol; certainly it is not the living and true God."

"Where the Spirit of the Lord is, there is freedom," said St. Paul. But the freedom planted and fostered by the word of God grows slowly and is not always as we imagined it. It does not spring up full-grown and without long care and work. It is more like that strong young tree that we nourish today with our struggle and care but which will offer abundant shade only to future generations. In nourishing the tree we already experience a beginning of liberation, enough to give meaning to a human life, to make one give oneself completely.

A SOURCE OF COMMITMENT TO THE POOR

I am going to reproduce some passages from a letter entitled "From a Farm Worker to the Christians of the Churches of Brazil." I will leave the passages just as they were written, with all the mistakes. This letter is a vivid example of the way reading the Bible nourishes in people the struggle for good against every form of oppression. It begins: "Today, September 15, I am writing you in this letter some terrible events of some inhuman facts and at the end of it I will say what I feel to be a Christian."

The letter goes on to describe, down to the tiniest details, some facts of injustice in which the tyranny of power left two farm workers defenseless and finally killed one of them. It continues:

Deer Christian it is true that in this letter I am denouncing these facts to the public and the oppressors every time they see this get angry and say we're communists evil mad and even persecute us they look for ways to trap us beat us but that's an old story, that happened with Christ. When he said to their face that those people of Israel wasn't helping them sick widows over there. Ref. Luke 5:25 and 27. When he said that they dragged him off to court headfirst Luke 4:28 and 29. When he talked about the injustices of the Pharisees they said this man is mad he's got a demon, they had a meeting to get him, but Jesus always told the truth and for telling the truth to defend the poor he got a lot of threats and he fled because he needed to struggle — he couldn't die without giving all his witness; that's why I'm writing I'm going to carry on denouncing in letters all the problem against the poor, but when my time comes I'll speak and prove the truth of the gospel without fear of dying because Jesus said As the Father sent me, so I send you John 20 verces 21. If this letter is read by any oppressors and they attack me as mad, I'll tell them it's you that's mad because you've no shame at doing this to the poor because Christ said whoever offends the least of his brother he's offending Christ. . . . I don't need to say my name I'm a farm worker and follower of Jesus the son of man who always struggled for liberation.

Courage directly nourished from the spring of the word of God. On the one hand, it was in his situation of oppression and in his struggle against the tyranny of power that the farm worker found the light to read and understand the Bible. Real life gave life and new meaning to the written word. On the other hand, the reading of that written word of the Bible encouraged him and guided him in his struggle for the liberation of his fellow human beings.

The poor look to the Bible to find meaning in life. If the Bible is "our book, written for us," then there must be a meaning *for us* in its text. It is relatively easy for the exegete to criticize the meaning the people find in this way and call it the product of imagination. Nonetheless the exegete's statement cannot negate the reality in this situation: a people gradually committing themselves to the liberation of their fellows. The Bible's meaning for us is real because it exists in practice in the lives of thousands of Christians, in the daily witness of their faith, nourished by constant reading and pondering on the Bible. It is very difficult for a person to die in defense of the meaning of the text in itself, a meaning discovered by the laborious research of exegetes. But many people have already died and many people are suffering and being imprisoned for defending the meaning which they themselves have discovered for their lives within the letter of the Bible, with or without the help of exegetes. And the certainty which the people acquire about the meaning they discover is not just any sort of certainty, not even a scientific certainty, but the certainty that God is speaking to them. Because of this they possess the courage to face even death, as is so clearly shown by the witness of the farm worker in his letter.

The reports show how seriously the people take Jesus' saying, "It isn't enough to hear the word; you must put it into practice."

A SOURCE OF FREEDOM AND NEW LIFE

Bacoral, a leper, still a boy, lives out in Acre, in the far western part of Brazil. The suffering and despair he has gone through in his life will never be described in books written by humans. At a meeting of evangelization group instructors, all lepers, he gave the following commentary on the gospel story of Our Lady's visit to St. Elizabeth:

I'm amazed. One poor woman visiting another simple woman, and they talk about salvation and the fate of the world! That happens here too. The gospel happens today. Here in this very meeting. But many people aren't simple and that's why they don't discover the great tasks awaiting them. You get people who go around saying, "I'm a friend of so-and-so," the doctor, the mayor, the senator, the landowner, or millionaire. They hang their greatness on the wrong hook. It's rubbish. What makes us valuable is that we're children of God! That's what I think.

While he was saying this, Bacoral was leafing through his copy of *Bíblia na Linguagem de Hoje* (The Bible in Today's Language). The disease had already eaten away part of his fingers, leaving only stumps.

According to Bacoral, the word of God reveals its power by giving dignity to and "resurrecting" the simplest and most afflicted people. Bacoral expressed his discovery in a song, with words and music both written by himself: "Like Jesus, I will carry my cross in order to rise again. Thank you, Lord, for teaching me to love, for love purifies me and makes me rise from the dead." His witness is proving the seed of new life for many other people who live with him in the leper hospital.

The same resurrection is alluded to in a question asked in another of the reports:

How is it that those who used to be despised are now, by their many great demonstrations of faith, challenging their former teachers? How is it that they now receive the greatest respect from the clergy, enjoy great autonomy in the church, and are rising, competent and strong, from a state of insignificance and inferiority which used to be regarded as constitutional, fatal, irremediable?

This theme occurs in a statement that I have quoted parts of above:

Now, with these Bible meetings and community meetings, we're beginning to realize that we're people. Many people don't realize what this means. There's so much injustice, and even more fear, even in the community. What really paralyzes you is fear. One person on her own can't cope and is afraid. These meetings are good because they help us to discover that we were made to be free. That's why I like, I've always liked, life in the church. I pray a lot — you should see me! As often as I can.

This woman, in simpler and shorter words, is saying just what I have said about the characteristics of the people's use of the Bible. She has covered all the points.

Still other statements take up this theme of the strength, liberation, and freedom that the people gain from the Bible:

The Bible, before, was undervalued by Catholics, and now you find that religion has changed a lot. The Bible, being read and not hidden, has made the people feel more liberated, freer, closer to the priest, even though they haven't studied like him.

Within the organization of the church the process of liberation can be seen in the fact that the people realize they're free and constantly appeal to the authority of the gospel when they feel crushed by the structures.

The reports tell of countless small struggles which people are waging against the forces which oppress and crush life. It is in all of this that resurrection is taking place and liberation is being made present.

Summary of the Strengths of Popular Interpretation

If we try to sum up the characteristics of the popular interpretation of the Bible, we find that it is a single reality with many facets. The Bible is used as a critical mirror of life; it is viewed as "our book, written for us"; the "letter" of the Bible is illuminated and given life by the light of faith in the people's eyes; the Bible is a source of commitment to the oppressed; it is a source of the resurrection and liberation of human life. Without the context of the people's lives and struggles, the context of resurrection, the text has neither power (Spirit) nor meaning (Word) nor author (God the Father).

This context of resurrection is not something spectacular. It is, rather, made up of the forces of hope in the people's lives: the simple happiness of being able to live with others in a community that is united for the service of others, of facing the challenge of a world at odds with God's plan and the dignity of human life, of trusting in God and the community's unity as a support in facing and one day overcoming the forces which oppose life in the world today.

All these characteristics of popular interpretation give an idea of the vision which is in the people's eyes when they start to read the Bible. This vision is not something taught but rather is something discovered; it has emerged from within the people, from their way of living the faith; it is something newly springing to life, and yet it is also very old; from the time of the New Testament and the Fathers of the church, it has always been a feature of Christian interpretation of the Bible.

Popular interpretation has many failings, defects, uncertainties, and ambiguities, as we shall see. However, the root is good, very much in accord with the *sensus ecclesiae*, the mind of the church, which has always guided the exposition of the Bible. It may then be of help to all of us, and to the church, to summarize and further reflect on the strengths of the popular interpretation of the Bible:

1. The Bible as a Mirror of Life. The main concern is not to find out what the Bible says in itself, but to learn what it has to say about life. For that reason it is seen as a "mirror." The Fathers of the Church had the same aim when they talked about allegory, symbol, type, shadow and image. They read the Old Testament in order to obtain a better understanding of the riches of the mystery of Christ which they were experiencing in the community of faith, the church. They always started from the "letter," but wanted to know what this "letter" had to say to Christians in the midst of their day-to-day lives.

2. "Our Book, Written for Us." What re-emerges here, in a new form, is the importance of what used to be called the *sensus ecclesiae*. Without the community it is not possible to come to a correct understanding of the Bible, for it is within the community that the Spirit who inspired the Bible acts; and since the Spirit inspired the Bible the Spirit is the only one who can reveal its true meaning. What re-emerges here, in a new form, is the ancient conviction that the Bible is the book of the people of God, and not just an instruction book on how to prove the truth of church teaching. It is the book of life.

3. *Seeing in the Light of Faith.* The Fathers looked for the "spiritual meaning." The spiritual meaning is not some pious or fantastic meaning, something dreamed up, but the meaning communicated by the Spirit to his church. A person who lives in the community that is the church lives in contact with the living, risen Christ, and receives from him the gift of the Spirit, who pulls the veil away from our eyes to reveal the meaning the Spirit wishes to offer to the church through the Bible: "The person who does not have the Spirit of God cannot receive the gifts which come from that very Spirit; they cannot even recognize them" (1 Cor. 2:14). Thus, that person cannot discover the spiritual meaning of the Bible.

4. *Leading to Commitment to the Poor.* The people's interpretation is not passive; it is active; it transforms. This was exactly the distinguishing feature of the Fathers' exegesis. In their eyes everything was, as it were, pregnant with the Holy Spirit, who was working within life and history enabling them to find their full meaning and flowering in Christ. Through their "spiritual exegesis" they sought to hasten the coming of the new dimension of human existence which appears in Christ. Interpretation is a way of transforming life to make it more in accord with the demands of the gospel.

5. *Liberation and Resurrection.* The people's interpretation of the Bible gives "inspiration" back its true meaning: for the people the Bible is not just a book which has authority to demand obedience because it is inspired by God, but also a book which brings God's inspiration into ordinary life. The Bible brings God's power to direct and transform existence, the same power which God used to free Christ from death. It brings liberation and resurrection because it attacks at the root the evil which vitiates human relationships and because it gives people a sense of being members of one family.

The People's Difficulties in Using the Bible

There used to be a sort of biblical fanaticism characterized by a blind faith in the word. Apart from that there was nothing.

Some people's way of living the power of faith in Jesus Christ often seems like a wig. It's put on for religious events and taken off for ordinary life. They're carnival masks and not the clear, cheerful and healthy faces of our people.

TRANSLATIONS OF THE BIBLE

There are a number of translations of the Bible, but not all of them are intelligible to everyone. Here in Brazil, it is much easier to produce a translation faithful to the original Hebrew or Greek text than to produce a translation faithful to the language of the poor people of this country. It is extremely difficult to translate the Bible into a language which can really be understood by the people. It is much easier to translate famous French or Italian translations. It is less work. For the people's benefit, though, it is much more urgent, and would be much more useful, to attempt a translation of the original text into a really popular language, even if the translation is imperfect. What are the criteria for a perfect translation? There aren't any, because they depend on the view each person has of the Bible and revelation. Maybe the most important is the people's good.

What is the point of an erudite and exact translation which people do not understand? Such a translation, even if strictly faithful to the original text, would not be faithful to the gospel. Faithfulness to the gospel demands also faithfulness to the people of today. "Fidelity to the people of today is difficult and demands effort, but it is necessary if we are to remain totally faithful to the message" (Paul VI addressing Italian exegetes).

There are some other points related to this issue that are apparently unimportant for a person used to dealing with books but that are very important for work with the people. A really popular edition of the Bible here in Brazil would need to have large, clear type. It would need to avoid complexity in layout; it would need to use very big and visible numbers to indicate chapters and verses and use very clear and punchy headings and subheadings. If possible, its size should also correspond to the scale of the Bible's importance in people's lives. It can never be forgotten that most people in study groups are people not used to reading. They have difficulty reading. Most of them have only elementary schooling. Some cannot see well, and in many places all they have to light up the pages of the Bible is an oil lamp.

THE TEXTS USED IN THE CELEBRATIONS AND MEETINGS

The three readings of the official liturgy are generally unintelligible to the people. Only a mind trained by lengthy courses in liturgy and theology can succeed in discovering even a possible connection between the three. The first Christians said, "Why impose on the converted pagans the burden of the law of Moses?" Today we might ask, "Why impose the burden of the three readings on the people?" To insist on this imposition is to forget that God wants us as free people, like children in our own home. Liturgy should be an experience in which we begin to live the freedom that God offers and that the people have to win. If the Bible and the liturgy themselves become an instrument for increasing the people's complexes about ignorance and dependence, how can we still talk about education for liberation?

THE READING OF THE TEXT

During a meeting of priests and farmers the gospel was read by one of the priests. He read clearly, pausing in all the right places. Then everyone was invited to comment. The priests spoke, but then no one else seemed to want to say anything. One of the priests, surprised at the peasants' silence, asked, "Aren't the farmers going to speak?" "Yes, we are," said one of them. "Well, now's your chance." "Read the gospel again," said the peasant. "We couldn't follow it."

This very common and very simple situation is a reminder of a very important and very complicated fact. The Bible began as a story of very straightforward facts and events, passed on by word of mouth for centuries, before being fixed in writing. Once fixed in writing, these stories became *readings*. But there is a very great difference between a reading and a story told without glancing at a written text.

In practice what we find is this. You can read a Bible text, even an easy, accessible text, and it may be read well, as the gospel was in our story. Despite all this you do not always manage to capture people's whole attention, and you often fail to make them understand the whole text. But as soon as you put down the written text and start saying the same thing in the form of a story, without a text in your hand, as though you were speaking your own words, immediately everyone listens and understands what you are saying.

Many of our people are more used to stories of this type than to readings. There are many remote areas where stories of this type are one of the main ways of passing on moral principles.

How can we take advantage of this in celebrations of the word or meetings? All those who want to replace a reading by a story must prepare what they are going to say very well. The effort put into preparation will, however, be generously rewarded by the results. A story told without reference to a written text immediately creates an atmosphere of communication rather than dependence. It draws people in much more than a straight reading. The solemn reading of the word can come at the end, after the reflection, like a closing rite. This is the place to remember a remark I quoted earlier: "A nervous, stumbling reading done by a member of the community has more of the flavor of liberation than a polished and educated reading by a priest or Sister."

CONQUERED BY THE "LETTER" OF THE BIBLE BUT NOT CAPTURED BY ITS MESSAGE

When people meet to discuss the Bible, often all they talk about is the literal meaning of the text, the "letter": they get trapped in it and lose their way. They fall into a literalism which turns the words on the page into something mystical and absolute. The Spirit, common sense, and creativity are stifled. These people are conquered by the "letter" of the Bible but not captured by its message. They become slaves of the Bible, oppressed by it, and the word of God brings them no liberation. The Bible remains covered with a veil (see 2 Cor. 3:14) and does not reveal its meaning. Many people even like this situation and defend it tooth and nail. It is their security, very often their only security.

Particularly in places where Catholics live side by side with fundamentalists and Jehovah's Witnesses, confusion over the "letter" becomes endless. The others accuse the Catholics of not following the Bible, because they smoke, dance, eat pork, eat meat with blood in it, do not keep the sabbath; Catholic women are criticized for wearing "men's clothes," such as long pants. In most cases the Bible contains prohibitions against these acts, in black and white. The Catholics do not know what to say and get confused, though in some cases common sense tells them that these rules are not to be taken literally.

I asked Dona Ormy from a rural part of the state of Minas, "What do you say when they come along with these problems?" She replied, "Me? I don't know what to say. I just tell them, 'Rubbish! You get on with your lives and I'll get on with mine!' " Right answer or wrong? Dona Ormy will never be able to make anything of the "literary form" and "cultural conditioning" which explain these statements in the Bible. She understands nothing of the distinctions introduced by exegetes to answer these questions. Her reasoning is very simple: "When my children are hungry, I'm not going to turn down the piece of suckling pig my neighbor offers me. I'm not going to refuse the long pants I can buy so cheap in the market for my daughter!" Following these and other criteria of experience, she reaches the same practical conclusion as the exegete. But many people do not have Dona Ormy's common sense or the education required to understand the exegete's reasoning, and so they get lost in a maze of confusion.

What sort of education will help people to correct the narrow and defective vision they have of the Bible without destroying the immense faith they have in the word of God? How can we ensure that the conclusions of modern exegesis about the literal meaning of the Bible are really put at the service of the poor and help them to free themselves from this near-suffocating attitude to the biblical text?

THE PEOPLE'S QUESTIONS ABOUT DIFFICULT BIBLICAL PHRASES

Once, at a meeting of thirty-eight leaders from base communities in rural areas of Ceará, I asked the following question: "What are the main difficulties you encounter in the Bible?" There was a moment of whispering, and then the group stated that they had had difficulties with the meaning of the following words and phrases: (1) Gentile, (2) scribe, (3) twelve tribes of Israel, (4) Levite, (5) Pharisee, (6) good Samaritan, (7) Pharaoh, (8) wise man from the East, (9) publican, and (10) priest (in the biblical era).

They were difficulties about individual words, quite specific and precise. The people were so sparing with words that they did not even use the plural where a singular would do. For that very reason I did not realize the full extent of the difficulty. I did not see straight away that each of these difficulties represented a particular incident which had taken place in one of their meetings. To give a useful answer I would have to know about the particular incident which gave rise to the question. The ten questions were like ten little doors or windows which the people opened to let us into their lives, but I did not realize my opportunity.

There is a great temptation to go straight to a good Bible dictionary and answer in terms of the material it contains. But is that the most useful way to respond to the problem presented by the communities? I don't know. What I do know is that each question has a double reference, one to the difficult text of the Bible, a text which remains outside us and provokes difficult questions in us, and another to the specific situation of the group or person which made the particular biblical phrase a problem. In order to be complete, the reply needs to take account of both references. To deal with the first, all you need is a dictionary, exegesis, information. To deal with the second, what is needed is solidarity and what Paul VI described as the "need to look for a certain connaturality of interests and problems with the subject matter of the text, if we are to be open to it and able to hear it" (address to Italian exegetes).

THE MEANING THE PEOPLE LOOK FOR IN THE BIBLE

Describing the procedure in the Bible study groups he took part in, Fábio, the owner of a small factory in Belo Horizonte, told us: "We do the following: we read a short piece of the gospel and then each one tries to say to the others what the text meant to them. It's not interpretation; we don't know anything about that. And we don't need interpretation. All we're trying to find out is what the gospel is saying to us in our lives. That's enough. If we started interpreting, we'd get completely mixed up, and the meeting would become complete chaos."

Fábio's remark should make interpreters think, be they exegetes, priests, or pastoral workers. The people have the idea that "interpretation" is a complicated and difficult business which is not of much use in real life. Where did they get this idea? From the exegetes themselves! Exegetes have made their work so complicated that it has begun to seem like a freeway, fenced off, so that mere pedestrians cannot use it: you can only use it if you have a fast car.

The result is that the people, who go on foot, continue their journey on a dirt track and use the Bible according to their lights. They reject the exegete's scientific explanation as unnecessary. There is a serious danger in all this. Popular interpretation may slide away from the demands of objectivity and fall into a spontaneous subjectivism and a naive and uncritical use of the Bible. This is the likely reflex of the naive and uncritical attitude many people have to life.

In many groups which meet to discuss the Bible the basic question is the same: "What message do you get from this text for your life?" Anyone who has ever taken part in such meetings knows that the reply is almost always the same, with small variations: "I admire Jesus' humility," or: "I find St. Peter's attitude a model of faith," and so on. People jump without any difficulty from the first century to the twentieth, as though the incident had occurred yesterday or the characters in the biblical story lived in the next block. The result is that they do not analyze Jesus' historical situation, and they draw conclusions which have no meaning for our day. Such a use of the Bible alienates the reader from his or her world.

Life and revelation demand much more than a simple, spontaneous, uncritical reading of the Bible. Faith never excuses us from the critical use of reason. Quite the opposite, it requires it, today more than ever. What practical help can exegesis offer to solve this real problem in pastoral work? In practice, the exegete's attitude to interpretation seems to be one thing, and the people's another. Both do their own thing in a different area, and they ignore each other. The people are looking for a meaning for their lives, while the exegete is more concerned with the text's meaning-in-itself. There is no integration of the two approaches. How can that integration be achieved?

NEED FOR A MORE CRITICAL AND JUDICIOUS USE OF THE BIBLE

One incident illustrates this point. On a radio program a group of Christians tried to inform the farmers in the diocese about the land problem in Brazil. With great realism, precision, and courage, they not only described the rights of rural workers, but also called on them to defend their rights by organizing and putting pressure on the authorities. At the end of the program they tried to explain the Christian dimension of this popular struggle and appealed to two biblical texts, that about the ten lepers and the one about the healing of the paralytic.

Of course there is nothing more biblical and Christian than helping oppressed people to win rights which have been denied them. In this case, however, the choice of texts and their application to the particular issue of land were not very helpful. In a sense, the Christians on the radio made the texts say what the program needed. They found a meaning-for-us which had no basis in the meaning-as-such of the texts. They were faithful to the Bible message in the first part of the program, when they did not talk about the Bible but only about the people's problems. In the second part they did not follow St. Peter's advice: "Always have your answer ready for people who ask you the reason for the hope you have" (1 Pet. 3:15). If you like, the fruit displayed in the first part was indeed from the biblical orchard, but when it came to saying what tree it had been picked from, they were at a loss. They offered and distributed beautiful oranges to the people and then pointed to a papaya tree and said, "They're from that tree." In such a case it is better to say nothing and simply distribute the fruit.

This raises once again the question of how to help the people to use the Bible to justify the biblical attitude they already have in their lives. In itself the justification by the Bible is secondary. What is really important is to support the people. What is important is to offer the oranges and distribute them. Nevertheless, because of questions other people will ask, and because of the demands of the faith today, it is increasingly necessary to use the Bible more critically and judiciously, in a way that corresponds to the demands of the real problems the people experience.

At the same time, never before has exegesis been so critical and so precise. More than ten thousand academic books and articles are published every year on biblical matters. But current exegesis, so far, is only critical with regard to the "letter" of the Bible and not as regards the application of its meaning to our lives. As a result, the immense critical system of modern exegesis gives little help in solving real pastoral problems. Reason enough for exegetes to make a serious examination of conscience about their function within the church.

The People's Method in Using the Bible

For us the method is essential. It gives meaning to the techniques of empowerment and is like a tool for extracting the content of the text. We believe in the people's capacities.

Nothing can justify destroying what has taken billions of years to create, with so much struggle. It is a precious inheritance from the past, which future generations have a right to know and enjoy.

CHARACTERISTICS OF THE METHOD THE PEOPLE USE TO INTERPRET THE BIBLE

It is important to bear in mind that the features described here will not be found everywhere. What I present below is more like an idealized picture, the fruit that will come if the tree is well looked after.

1. Reading the Gospel in the Context of Life. This is the most widespread feature. One report on a community said the group begins with "a real-life incident, usually a collective experience or something that took place in the town, whether at work, in the neighborhood, in school, or in the families. Then there are questions to get the people to see how common the situation is, and to see the causes which produce situations like that. Then we read a Bible text and immediately afterward there's another series of questions which help the people to see better God's plan and set out on specific action." Everything is done in this way so that "life may be the place of commitment, reflection and encounter with Christ." This concern to read the gospel in the context of life is often not explicit, but it is the premise of the people's whole use of the Bible. It is like the root from which everything else grows.

2. *Everyone Learns from Life and from the Gospel.* "Nothing is imposed, but everything that comes from the group is accepted. There are neither teachers nor students, because all regard themselves as learning from life and from the gospel. There's no attempt to give answers, but we try to formulate the problem properly. The more aware people say they feel oppressed when someone acts as the teacher: they're not interested in a teacher who wants to impart wisdom to them. But they do value a fellow student with more education, someone they can talk to on an equal basis." The same thing is stressed in a very suggestive phrase I have quoted a number of times before: "to exchange ideas so as to discover the Holy Spirit's idea among the people."

3. *Before, During, After.* A report from one community made the following statement about the relation between the Bible, action, and reflection: "Reflection on life and action, before, during, and after, has brought us to a comprehensive view of the social situation and a high degree of awareness. After every step we take we meet to consider the successes and failures. All reflection starts from the reading of the gospel, and comparing it with our lives. This method is liberating in the vision and awareness it gives of the world, in the understanding it gives of problems and their causes and consequences, in the commitment it creates within and outside the community, in the questions it constantly provokes: 'Is this what Jesus Christ wants of us?' or 'Is this the Father's will?', and in the discovery of the person of Christ, who is a real power in everything."

4. *Analysis of Society.* This is what three reports on the communities said about the Bible and social analysis: "A comparison between the gospel ideal and the very different situation in society has provided an atmosphere and concepts for an analysis of the causes of oppression as a system. It is a dynamic analysis, nourished and confirmed by everyday events." "As an antidote

to one sort of alienating reading of the Bible, we have made some attempts at an incarnational or political reading." This educational method is liberating "because it makes available tools which enable the people to analyze their situation and criticize alienating religious presuppositions when they have to deal with the Bible and real-life problems. Some people said, 'We were blaming God for this bad situation, but now we've discovered that the fault was ours because we hadn't been doing anything to change it.' "

5. *An Attitude of Inquiry.* "The method consists in regarding the people as the controllers of their destiny, with a firm confidence in the active presence of the Spirit among them. From this point of view, investigation is an indispensable tool for discovering this presence of the Spirit, and that discovery is begun by starting from the needs the community feel to be most pressing. Systematically feeding back the data obtained from the investigations is an enormous incentive to discussion of problems and plans for action." As the following statement reveals, it is always necessary that analysis be rooted in the gospel and the people: "The pastoral workers began to investigate the situation, and realized that on their own they could do nothing. They reported this study back to the people, making comparisons with the gospel and intensifying the study of the situation. Gradually the people made commitments and formed groups."

6. *The People's Common Sense and Natural Wisdom.* The reports are full of remarks from the people which illustrate how easily they compare gospel situations with real-life situations. Greater attention to this popular culture as a medium of biblical interpretation may help to correct the mistakes which exist in the use of the Bible and may even reveal some faults which we cannot even see yet. Using the people's common sense and natural wisdom as an entrance point to the texts has enabled exegetes and the people to break free of a rigid and literal view of the Bible. The people have gradually lost their biblical fanaticism, and reading the Bible has also made them aware of the political dimension of faith.

7. *Unity Is Strength.* One of the reports stated: "During our dialogue the idea came up: we meet around the gospel to understand it; why not make an effort to put it into practice?" As

a result of that practice, community awareness then grows. That is, there is a reciprocal and mutually nourishing relation between common action and reflection in community; and from that relation comes strength borne of unity: "Out of reflection in the group there grows action which is no longer individual but communal, and from a small-scale activity, evaluated and analyzed to examine what went wrong, we discover the need to organize better to create strength, which helps us to struggle in other areas and control the process of action itself. The people become the initiators of their history and less and less manipulated." Other ways of saying the same thing: "When one of us feels pain we are all hurt." "We learn to defend ourselves in contact with others."

8. Gradual Independence. On the theme of independence various reports stated: "At present the laity of the diocese are organizing at all levels and holding local, regional, and diocesan meetings on their own initiative. 'Laity' has meant those who work at the lowest level, but the word is recovering its real meaning: member of the people." "We are coming to understand that the church is us; we better understand the meaning of church when we attempt to improve our conditions and the conditions of all the people of our community." "The educational approach is liberative because the most advanced communities are becoming more and more independent of those who support them and able to take initiatives directly with the people, after they have critically examined their own situation." In this way there is a growing sense of shared responsibility.

9. A Transforming Interpretation. The last point I should stress is the people's concern not merely to hear but also to practice the word of God. Through their interpretation they try not only to understand things but also to change what is not in accord with the gospel. The interpretation is not passive, but active. This is the key point at which popular interpretation differs from traditional interpretation as learned in seminaries.

THE PEOPLE'S METHOD AND THE METHOD OF EXEGESIS

1. The Method of Exegesis. In its attempt to discover the historico-literal meaning, modern exegesis follows the method of coherence and reasoning. That is, it follows a rigid and coherent logic in assembling its ideas. The persons who use the method of coherence are clear about all they do and say. They make no statement which cannot be justified.

It is a form of reasoning whose strengths are objectivity and the exactitude of its concepts. It constructs a biblical synthesis, systems, and theologies. It is strong and weak at the same time. It is like a well-built house in which all the bricks have their own place according to the architect's calculations, but also in which there is one girder that if removed, everything collapses and the synthesis is worthless. Each element is important and has its quite precise place in the overall logic. In the search for the historico-literal meaning this is the method which has to be used. There is no other.

Pastoral workers use something of this method of coherence and logic. In their heads they have a particular vision or plan which has to be implemented within the people's world. Consequently, at the beginning pastoral work usually goes in a straight line, that is, taking ideas to the people in accordance with the logical plan in our heads. But are we ready to rethink our method and correct our plan when the flower which springs from the people, and which we have watered, turns out to be different from the idea we had of it?

2. The People's Method. The people's method in using the Bible does not stress internal coherence or reasoning, but is more like a free association of ideas. People talk freely and put together ideas, facts, and situations, as they occur to them, without a visible logical connection.

"Our people's environment doesn't place much stress on concepts. They may even lack clear ideas of the official church's system of beliefs. But no one doubts that their universe is saturated with faith, however inadequate the expression of this faith may be, as it grapples with unassimilated (and unassimilable) concepts. The word comes to life for them, hot with relevance, throbbing with life, dense with particularity. This accounts for the ease with which they invent expressions, the freedom of the associations, the richness of the images, the freedom of speech and gesture, reflecting the way, for them, word and action form a unity."

To priests or exegetes who know only the method of coherence and logic, such an interpretation based on free association of ideas and images may seem to lack all logic, coherence, or substance. The people seem to want to build houses with bricks laid anyhow, without a plumb line or mortar or plan, with no system. But this is only the impression we have because we judge the people by our criteria. In fact, the people are not trying to build houses: that is, they are not trying to develop rational systems or syntheses; they are not trying to construct "theologies" of this or that; at least, that is not the purpose of their method. The people's method is different: it has a different root, follows a different path, and has a different objective because underlying it there is a different vision of life and the Bible.

We, the exegetes and the priests, are very worried about the intellectual content of the faith. We are worried about *orthodoxy*. The exegete wants to know the meaning of the text in itself, the historical basis of faith. The path the exegete takes to reach this goal is the historical, literary, and philological one. The people's method does not seek to refine the intellectual content of faith, but works to reinvigorate its root, so that it may bear fruit in life. The people are less interested in knowing the meaning as such of the text than in discovering the meaning it has for their lives today. They want to know what God has to say to us today through the Bible. They want to know God's will in order to put it into practice. They are concerned with *orthopraxis*.

The root of the people's thinking is better than the root which gives rise to the method of traditional exegesis learned in the seminaries. The intellectual content of the people's ideas may have its deficiencies, but a much greater danger is correct content growing from and nourished by a poisoned root. That kind of content is a fruit that offers no life-giving nourishment.

The Root of the People's Method

The people's method is like a tree. Its branches are separate, poke up into the air, all coming from the same trunk, but growing freely with no apparent order or direction but mutually balanced by an invisible force. They receive unity, life, solidity, and strength from the invisible root which spreads under the ground. You can cut off a branch, or pull off a leaf, and the tree does not fall or die, but carries on living and producing fruit. The exegete can criticize some of the people's interpretations and dismiss them as arbitrary, but that does not make the tree die. The root from which all this springs is not visible, but it is present in all the branches and leaves.

The people's method is not a reflective one. They have a clear awareness of everything they say and do, but they are not always aware of the motive force of their interpretation. Still that forces branches out in the ground of life, where the Spirit acts—the same Spirit who, in the past, brought the text of the Bible into being.

For discovering the historico-literal meaning the method of coherence and logic is better. But for discovering the meaning the people are looking for—that is, the meaning which the Holy Spirit is offering us today through the text of the Bible—the people's method is much more efficient and has a great deal to teach the exegete and the priest. Anyway, it is a much older method than the method of modern exegesis. It is the method which characterized the exegesis of the Church Fathers. The logical method is not suitable for picking up the voice of the Spirit. All it can pick up is the voice of the "letter." But "the written letters kill, while the Spirit gives life," as St. Paul said.

All this can be compared to the process of gestation and birth. The moment a child is conceived, a whole natural mechanism comes into operation which leads to the child's birth. God's future is gestating among the people, the embryo of a new vision of life. The mechanism for bringing this new future into the world has already started operating. This dynamic mechanism is the people's method.

Like the mother-to-be, the people do not know the features of the offspring they are carrying. They do not have clear ideas. Their method is more intuitive, less precise in the formulation of the boundaries of revealed truth, but much more suggestive in enabling others to imagine the source from which all truth and faith derives, more suited to suggesting something of the indescribable mystery of God and of life.

That is why it is vitally important to pay close attention to the people's timid attempts to verbalize this new experience, which is the shape of the future, gestating and tiny. Through the people's method of free association, a new vision of life is looking for a path to blossom in consciousness and in life itself. The strength and power of the people's method are not in the content of the things they say, but in the embryo that is striving to be born. The strength and power are not in the logical coherence, but in the practical coherence with which they live their faith. In this way they are bringing to birth the child which the Spirit conceived in them. By their use of the Bible, the people are trying to hasten the birth, to bring joy to the world at the birth of this new being. For the present, the people writhe in the pains of labor. They herald the birth in simple words and images, trying to express their inexpressible experience: "An 'I know not' which is left stammering" (St. John of the Cross).

BETWEEN OBJECTIVISM AND SUBJECTIVISM

The fear of falling into the people's subjectivism has led exegetes to the other extreme — the objectivism of the meaning of the text-in-itself. Their concern with the objectivity of things has made it impossible for other Christians to take part in the interpretation of the Bible. The people understand little of the issues debated by the academics discussing the historico-literal meaning. In this way, despite all its goodwill and its undeniable merits, scientific exegesis has hidden the key of the Bible (see Mt. 23:13) and provoked the natural and understandable reaction of a misplaced, exaggerated, and spiritualistic exegesis among uneducated people who say, "If we started interpreting, we'd get completely mixed up, and the meeting would become complete chaos." In turn, those people, adopting a dangerous subjectivism, confirm the exegetes in their anxiety to make the whole content of faith objective and define it scientifically, in order to place it out of reach of arbitrariness. It seems a vicious circle.

We have not succeeded in achieving Pius XII's ideal of "the happy and fruitful union between the doctrine and spiritual sweetness of expression of the ancient authors and the greater erudition and maturer knowledge of the modern" (*Divino Afflante Spiritu*). Nonetheless this integration is more necessary today than ever.

On the one hand we have the uncontrolled explosions of Pentecostalism on all sides, and the rise of charismatic movements which appeal to popular religious feeling instead of critical reason. The members of these movements want to escape from all norms and authority, invoking the freedom of the Spirit. Because of the all-pervasiveness of mass media, there is also a need for an interiorization of the things of faith and life; without that interiorization people risk losing their identity and becoming almost unable to find themselves. Our culture of massification and oppression has left the individual very fragile. All this shows, in one way or another, the emptiness of our present culture and the urgent need for a community religious experience of the living and true God, an experience which will give strength, direction, and a new meaning to life.

On the other hand we have the complexity of the problems of modern life. Science poses serious questions for faith. There is a need for a more critical and less naive view of life, as the forces of oppression, repression, and marginalization constantly refine their techniques. All this is showing that charisms, the breath of the Spirit, and goodwill are not enough. There is a need for planned action, a strategy for evangelization, an organization of the people's hope, a critical vision of faith and the Bible, and a clear understanding of the political dimension of Christian charity for the struggle against the forces which are destroying human life.

This, in my view, is the challenge our world presents to those who explain the Bible to the people. Information, knowledge, and sound doctrine are not enough. We have to involve experience and reach the source which once spurred knowledge, gave us the doctrine, and generated historical information. In this regard the people's method has a lot to teach exegetes and priests.

But experience and blind faith are not enough. They have to be organized by reason with a view to the conversion and transformation of life and society. It is no use having a wonderful electrical system at home without the power which comes from the generator. The power from the generator is no use without the network of wires to conduct it. In other words, the power and the system need each other—the methods of modern exegesis and of the human sciences should complement the people's method. Thus, as regards the use of the Bible in the church, the solution is not to choose between scientific exegesis and the people's method; rather the solution is to employ both methods to uncover the core of the gospel.

In attempting to establish this complementarity, one of the main problems is the freedom of the people's method and the abundance of interpretations that it generates. The people's suitcase has, so to speak, become so full that it has burst the official locks of scientific exegesis and official faith. It will not shut any more. The contents are spilling out. The people who notice this first are not the locksmiths—the representatives of the faith, the bishop, or the representative of science, the exegete—but the parish priests and pastoral workers who have the job of getting the suitcase to shut. Some of them would like to clear out the suitcase and throw away half the contents, but that is not possible because the people will not allow it. Others are looking for stronger locks, and another group is looking for a bigger suitcase. They knock on the doors of the bishop and the exegete. The people themselves do not seem very bothered by this problem. They are free. They do not depend on the suitcase. Instead of the two locks of scientific exegesis and official faith, they use the two ropes of common sense and the simple faith they received from their parents. What will not fit in the suitcase is put in bags and boxes. Real life does not fit in the suitcase we handed to the people!

Neither the people's method nor the method of exegesis should be regarded as perfect. The problem is that the two, which should be united, are in fact separate. Each interprets the Bible in its own way, to the detriment of both. Without mutual guidance, each is in danger of losing its way. Popular interpretation, for lack of help from scientific exegesis, is in danger of slipping into subjectivism. The interpretation of exegesis, for lack of contact with life, is in danger of seizing up completely and getting lost in the meanderings of its own speculations, turning the exegete into a technocrat of the Bible.

THE FOUR STAGES OF THE REAPPROPRIATION OF THE BIBLE BY THE PEOPLE

A widespread movement of "rediscovery and reappropriation of the Bible by the people" is currently under way. Though it takes different forms in each place, this movement in general can be divided into four stages. The purpose of describing these four stages is to help the reader to understand better what is happening and provide an instrument with which to analyze what is really taking place in this aspect of the use of the Bible by the people.

1. Before the Present Change. Previously the Bible, regarded as "the book of the church," was interpreted and explained to the people by the clergy in accordance with the church's rules. This general description, "explaining the Bible in accordance with the church's rules," continues to be permanently valid, today perhaps more than ever. What is changing is the form this process takes.

Previously the interpretation of the Bible as taught in seminaries was at the service of the doctrinal system then in force. It was part of the distribution of "knowledge" to the "ignorant" people. To say "the Bible is the book of the church" was synonymous with saying "the Bible is the book of the hierarchy." The high-level renewal of exegesis of the last two hundred years did not question this situation. In one sense it reinforced it, transferring the teaching role to exegetes, who become in practice the controllers of knowledge about the Bible. They ended up creating an inferiority complex and a feeling of ignorance, not only among the people, but also in priests and bishops. Many of the clergy became frightened to talk about the Bible.

As a result of the prevailing view of the Bible and its function in the church and in the lives of Christians, the criteria of interpretation were almost exclusively historical and literary (and also implicitly doctrinal). The real human situation as ordinary people experienced it did not come into the frame of reference for determining the meaning of the Bible. One of the reports explained that in pastoral practice this system took the following form: "There was no room in the church for poor people. The church had room only for the powerful, those who were stronger. Poor people had no right even to speak, because they had to be quiet as soon as the priest raised his voice."

2. The Restoration of the Bible to the People. The Bible began to be returned to its true owners, the people. For example, in Brazil millions of copies were published and sold. The Protestant Bible societies have already distributed more than two billion copies around the world, and have translated the Bible into more than 1200 languages.

The Catholic hierarchy and the clergy encouraged this distribution and invited the exegetes to distribute something of their knowledge to the people and help to get the Bible message understood. As a result biblical courses sprang up on all sides, Bible weeks and the first "Bible circles." A whole new popular literature appeared with the goal of distributing in manageable portions the new scientific discoveries about the literal and historical meaning of the Bible. The purpose of this was to inform the people, to enable them to be better acquainted with the content of the Bible.

This exegetical literature produced a *new* vision which made the Bible an *old* book, because it pushed the Bible back into the past, that is, into the historical and literary context in which it originated. This is a detrimental effect of the popularization of the results of academic exegesis among the people. This exegesis leads people to forget their present and return to the biblical past and venerate strange stories of former times which will never return. In this journey of theirs back to the biblical past the people are totally dependent on the exegete, the guide, who takes them through the world of the Bible. Academic interpretation, however, on its own, does not have the power to return the Bible and the people to the present, from which historical investigation diverted them.

3. The Rediscovery of the Bible by the People. The people, once in possession of the Bible but uninterested in literary and historical discussions, began to read the Bible according to a new principle, the only one available to them: they began to read the Bible and compare it with their lives. This simple and unpretentious reading, without much "scientific" worth, led them to discover a new dimension of the Bible, an authentic dimension, but one which was forgotten and largely disregarded by modern exegesis. The people are beginning to see in the Bible not only an account of past history but also a reflection of the current history of which they are a part.

This rediscovery of the Bible as a "mirror of life" is beginning to restore to the people their identity as the people of God. It is by looking in the mirror of the Bible that the people are rediscovering their human face and their mission in the world.

By discovering in the Bible the mirror of their lives, the people enable the Bible to occupy, at last, the place it seeks to occupy in life and history. "God's letter" has reached the right address. Through this reinsertion into the people's life, the Bible is now in a position to begin operating and producing its fruits.

4. The Reappropriation of the Bible by the People. Now the people recognize the Bible as their book, the "book of the church," of the people of God, "written for us." It is no longer a book which belongs to the hierarchy alone, but is the possession of all who belong to the people of God.

The Bible, seen and read in this way, begins to "inspire" life, reviving a different vision of both itself and of life, a vision centered on the living and experienced presence of the person of Christ and on faith in the action of the Holy Spirit. It is a very old vision now awakening in the people, but one which makes the Bible a new and relevant book because it brings it into the present, inserts it into the people's life, and transforms it into the hidden motor of the current process of renewal. Seen in terms of this vision, the strange old stories of the Bible begin to have a striking modernity and invite study.

As a result, this new vision of the Bible and life gives rise to new structures and methods of interpretation, which come into conflict with the older structures and methods, and call them radically into question as they show their limitations.

The earlier methods of exegesis sought to distribute a knowledge which came from outside. The new ones seek to extract the new vision which is awakening among the people and make it explicit in action. The previous methods were ways of putting into practice a theory devised by others; the new ones are ways of getting the flower to unfold from the bud. Their aim is to enable the new vision present within current action to develop and clarify, and also to enable the theory arising out of this action to become in its turn a critical instrument to guide and refine this action.

These four stages now exist simultaneously and intermingled, in our heads and in practice. We are still waiting for a fifth stage in which the current process will find its direction; we are waiting for exegesis to discover the limits of its method, redefine its procedures, and use its knowledge, no longer as something which is an end in itself, but as a real service to the people. On the other hand, as we have already seen, for want of more academic support, the people's use of the Bible may wander off and get lost in the byways of incoherent subjectivity, like the branch of an orange tree which breaks under the weight of the fruit for want of a stake to support it.

OLD VISION, NEW BOOK

The people's method is "a tool which extracts the content." What is the content? I firmly believe that in this simple activity of the people, so ambivalent, so full of failings and uncertainties, so fragile, we are seeing the awakening of the same vision of the Bible and life which, in the distant past of the church, gave rise to what is known as spiritual exegesis. Spiritual exegesis seeks to capture what the Spirit is saying (hence its name), the meaning the Spirit is offering to people today.

Spiritual exegesis seems a beautiful theory, interesting but without substance, as Chinese acupuncture seems to Western medicine. Western medicine is still groping for principles to understand and assess the value of acupuncture for us. And yet acupuncture existed long before the birth of Western medicine.

In the same way, spiritual exegesis is so distant from modern exegesis that modern exegesis perhaps cannot even see the possibility that it may have value for us in Brazil or for people in other parts of the world. Yet spiritual exegesis existed long before the emergence of modern exegesis, and it is foreign only for those who are locked into the dominant system of today. It is not foreign for the people, among whom it has been reborn, for the moment, without a label and without much method, a mixture of chaff and wheat.

The truth is that there exists in the church a practical wisdom which comes from the distant past. It is revealed and preserved in the day-to-day practice of the faith, in which the Bible is read, pondered, and interpreted by the people in the light of their practical problems. Referring to this process in the epigraph to this chapter, I used these words: "Flower, you turn blood into fertilizer! / You are stronger than the hand which cuts you, / More enduring than the idea which defines you, / Brighter than the paint which portrays your face. / The world is growing afraid of you, / Defenseless flower!" In other words, in the real practice of Christians the Spirit is speaking through the Bible, offering them a meaning for their lives. While academics become wrapped up in the past, trying to define how and when the Spirit speaks, the people listen to what the Spirit is saying to them now and try to put it into practice. *Practice is more advanced than theory.*

It is one thing to interpret the Bible as a Christian, and another to be able to define the principles of this interpretation. It is one thing to have blood flowing in your veins and another to know how blood flows in veins. All people, even the poorest and most ignorant, have blood flowing in their veins. Only scholars and specialists in the subject know how blood flows in veins, and in order to find out about this they have to study the bodies of living people and not just the corpses of people who have died.

Perhaps academics and scholars should become less pretentious and more humble, less expert, and become pupils of the current practice of the church, particularly of the poorest, to whom God is revealing things which they have certainly not heard from the "learned" and the experts. In a very simple way, almost through an intuition of their faith, these people have recovered the vision of the Bible and of life which in the past gave rise to spiritual exegesis.

Today we are in a phase of "re-reading." The previous doctrinal and rational synthesis, with all its spin-offs, many of which still fill our heads today, is no longer adequate to contain the new life which is springing up all over the place. From the ordinary people, the seedbed of faith and life, we see being reborn today, at the prompting of the Spirit, ideas which enable us to criticize the old synthesis and construct a new one more in accord with what God is asking of us.

THE CENTRAL PROBLEM: UNDER WHAT CONDITIONS DOES THE BIBLE LIBERATE?

When a problem arises in the community, we choose a good reading for the celebration and discuss the problem with everyone during the celebration.

We are trying through reading the Bible to get people to look at their lives with the guidance and light of the gospel, and as far as possible to steer people into community action.

The particular church, in communion with the church of the Third World, because of the gospel and responding to the challenge of the local situation, takes a stand for and with the oppressed and, as a result, defines its pastoral work as liberating evangelization.

Who Sowed the Tares among the Wheat?

Why should it be that in some places the use of the Bible is awakening the people to renewal while in other places it seems to produce the opposite effect?

It is not enough to say, "We're going to promote the Bible, and the power of God's word will do the rest." And it is not enough to say, "We're going to instruct the people about the Bible, and the rest will follow automatically." After all, there are places where the Bible was more or less the center of everything, where faith in the word of God could not have been greater, where every month there was instruction about the Bible, and where the word of God still did not reveal its power and the people became closed in a biblical fanaticism very similar to that of the fundamentalist sects. Attachment to the Bible can become biblicism and, as we have seen already, members of some "Bible circles" can sometimes be the most conservative, most inhibited, and least free group in the parish.

It may even happen that the celebrations of the word become more beautiful and lively, more religious and fanatical, as the alienation and poverty of the people increases. Many people read the Bible in the light of their religious feelings. They use the Bible to take off on flights of religious experience and as a result arrive sometimes at heroic attitudes of solidarity and sometimes at an alienation so great that the interpreter has the feeling of talking to an impenetrable wall.

In other places, however, the word of God is revealing its power and producing positive results:

Those who were once despised are now, through their many great exploits of faith, challenging their former teachers, receiving the utmost attention from the parish priest, enjoying autonomy within the church, and are capably and firmly raising themselves from a state of insignificance and inferiority. . . . They read the Bible in the liturgy and outside it. From it they draw stories of God's action, principles of deep wisdom, the mysteries of Christ, and his vision of the kingdom. They discuss these treasures together, relating them with their everyday lives, and in the process the first revolution takes place, one which is Pentecostal, fundamental: each person moves from a knowledge received to a knowledge discovered.

Indeed, everything said so far about the use of the Bible by the people has shown how the Bible is the hidden motor of all renewal in the church.

In one place participation in Bible meetings led the people to the conclusion that "some people's knowledge can no longer be a privilege which sets them apart and above others, but should simply be a service like all others." Those who were privileged to have knowledge and who wanted to be a part of the renewal had to undergo a deep conversion. As a result many left the movement. In this way the use of the Bible produced a judgment with a good result. In another place, however, the use of the same Bible produced exactly the opposite effect: "The people who talk most and most easily are the most highly regarded. People judge more by words than actions." This led to an oppressive educational method in which the participants were left dependent on those who knew more and were able to express it. From these examples we can see that the Bible either helps or hinders; it either liberates or oppresses. It is not neutral. It saves or kills.

There are many tares growing among the wheat. Who sowed them? What is it that enables the Bible to have its effect and produce its fruits of freedom?

The Three Forces at Work When the Bible Is Explained to the People

To use the Bible well we need more than the Bible; we need to do more than study the text. There are three forces which come into operation when we try to explain the Bible to the people: the force of the particular problem burdening the people's lives, the force of the scientific investigation carried out by exegesis, which questions established certainties, and the force of the church's faith awakening in the "memory" of Christians.

Life, science, and faith. People, exegesis, and church. Three forces in constant tension, each with its defenders, attempting in its own way to make its contribution to the correct use of the Bible in the church. I repeat: these are *forces,* not just ideas, historical forces, much stronger than we are.

THE PEOPLE'S LIVES

This means the situation we are living in today, in all its dimensions, which confronts us with certain questions: religious, family-related, cultural, social, economic, and political questions. It means our people with their characteristics. It means the life we all live. In a word, it is the *pre-text,* that is, all that preexists in us, before we come into contact with the text, and which leads us to look in the text for a *meaning for life.*

SCIENTIFIC EXEGESIS

The critical approach of scientific exegesis permeates Christian thought today and has already brought about many changes in the way we look at the Bible and life, has already overthrown many beliefs and helped to eliminate many doubts. It includes reason, logic, and love for truth, which examine and question everything, which refuse to accept just any explanation, and which strive to elucidate what is authentic in the texts. It includes common sense and natural wisdom which make us suspicious of so much. It includes the text of the Bible when read and interpreted by the criteria of science, independently of any preconceived idea, in order to discover its *literal meaning.*

THE CHURCH'S FAITH

The church's faith is the particular vision with which Christians approach the Bible, seeking in it a direct dialogue with God. It is the church these days engaged in renewal, putting the Bible into the hands of the people. It is the faith of the community which receives and reads the Bible as its book, which functions as the *context* in the reading of the text. It is the Spirit of God, the divine author of the Bible, who pulls away the veil from the reader's eyes and so gives life to the written letters and, through them, *a new meaning to God's people.*

The Triangle

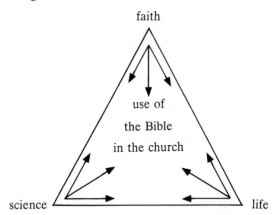

These forces and the interplay between them can be likened to a triangle. From each angle there is a complete view of the whole inside field of the triangle. As a result there is an inherent tendency for each of the three forces to overestimate its function, make its own point of view absolute, shut itself up in the search for its meaning, forget that it is only one part of a larger whole, and think that it is capable, by itself, with its own analytic principles, of explaining all the phenomena which appear inside the triangle.

This is just what happened. One of the three forces, exegesis, got the upper hand, took over interpretation, and the two other functions were left behind. Faith and life were left without any particular function, more or less subordinate to scientific exegesis. Just look at some introductions to the Bible. They leave no room for life or faith. The only valid approach is the scientific analysis of the texts.

In this way the balance of the fruitful tension which should exist between the three forces was broken. Each of the forces — scientific exegesis, dogmatic exegesis, and popular pietistic exegesis — went its own way, interpreting the Bible for its own purposes. The overall structure was destroyed. This imbalance does violence to reality. When the context is the use of the Bible in the church, it is impossible for any one force to isolate itself from the other two without the risk of fragmenting itself and losing its identity. The diagram of the triangle illustrates this very well. The two lines, for example, which form the angle of faith come from the heart of the angles of science and the people's life. In each angle the three forces are present, must be present, and must be inseparable. If we separate them, we destroy the correct use of the Bible and prevent the manifestation of the liberating power of the word of God.

The problem of the use of the Bible in the church can be formulated in the following way. We have to ensure that the meaning discovered in the Bible: (1) corresponds to the demands of the people's situation; (2) corresponds to the demands of a scientific analysis of both text and situation; and (3) is at the same time the direct revelation of the Holy Spirit's appeal to God's people. If one of these three elements is missing, our interpretation is defective, or at least incomplete. In other words, the *text* has to be read and interpreted in the light of the *pre-text* of life and within the *context* of the community's faith. It is like a violin. The text is the strings, the context is the sound-box, and the pre-text is the reason for playing and the audience which asks for a cheerful tune. Without the audience, without a reason for playing, without the sound-box, all that is left are strings, which on their own will not produce music.

The Heart of the Problem

The greatest problem in interpreting the Bible in our day is not finding a better interpretation of this or that text; nor is it using faith criteria a little more; nor is it stimulating the people's creativity so that they discover a meaning for their lives in each text. Interpreting the word of God does not depend just on exegesis or on infallible academic competence on the part of the exegete; it does not depend just on faith or a better knowledge of the church's tradition; it is not reliant solely on everyday life or more intense solidarity with the people. It depends on the integration of all these three forces.

In general all the training of an interpreter of the Bible, whether exegete, priest, or pastoral worker, is limited to a study of the biblical text. Underlying this training seems to be the idea that those who use the Bible well are those who are good at explaining the text-in-itself, the literal meaning. But that is not true. Without the background of the Spirit (context) and without the context of the people's life-situation (pre-text), the text of the Bible remains a dead letter, just on paper. What we lack is not knowledge about the text. In some ways we know too much. What we really lack is the ability to integrate the study of the Bible into the community's faith-life and into the life-situation of the people; we are going to have to develop this skill if we are going to enable the text to recover a life and reveal a meaning to us. At present we lack this skill because it has never been taught to us. We are going to have to start learning.

The heart of the problem is to enable the faith community (context) and real life (pre-text) to occupy once more their rightful place within the overall process of interpreting the Bible.

If we analyze the various difficulties and dead ends encountered both in the people's use of the Bible and in our explanation of the Bible to the people, we find that the cause lies in the imbalance of these three forces. Either the violin is played for no reason, just for the sake of playing, without an audience; or it is played without a sound-box; or it will not play because the strings are broken. Biblical fanaticism, attachment to the "letter," conservative fundamentalism, moralism and conformism, refusal to look beyond liturgy, alienated religious attitudes, tendentious (dogmatic or ideological) use of the text, naive and uncritical subjectivism, dominating interpretation, use of the text to mystify — all these occur for one of three reasons: either people fail to understand the text, or they forget to look at the pre-text of real life, or there is no context. And we also find that the biggest problems, that is, the very ones which turn the Bible into an oppressive book and prevent the people from waking up, derive not from ignorance about the text, but from the absence of a faith-context and, above all, from lack of attention to the pre-text of real life.

We have to start learning afresh how to read and interpret the Bible properly. However, this learning cannot be done merely by reading books about the problem, that is, at the level of ideas, because, as I said before, the problem is not ideas but rather historical forces much stronger than us. We have to go and see, go where the forces of faith and life are awakening once more, trying to recover their place. And this is happening among the ordinary people.

It is ordinary people, stimulated by real-life problems, who have begun to read the Bible. The conflict, previously latent, is beginning to be put into words and deepened. An integration of the three forces is already under way, within the new forms of activity starting up all around us. We are not doing it with our discussions. They only make explicit what we are able to pick up from the life around us. They seek to catch the direction of the wind of history, God's history, and to be faithful to it.

Two Comparisons to Illustrate the Matter

THE MAN WHO SLEPT FOR A HUNDRED YEARS

The use of the Bible in the church is like the man who slept for more than a hundred years inside his own house. When he awoke he could no longer find his proper place, except the bed he had slept in all this time. He knew no one. The new residents of his house were the descendants of his grandchildren, all born after he had fallen asleep. They were strangers to him. They did not recognize him awake, but only unconscious, sleeping in the bed, not disturbing anyone by his presence.

But now, all of a sudden, everything changed for everyone! Once awake, the old owner tried to go on exercising his role of householder as before. He had no other role model. The new residents, however, would not let him. They did not want to lose the rights they had won.

The old owner was left with only two alternatives: either he could completely adapt to the new situation and renounce his old rights, or he could look for a corner in the house where he could continue to be the owner without upsetting the others. Neither of the two solutions was ideal, but a third which respected the rights of both parties had still to be found.

Both the man himself and his descendants, all very honorable people, today live under pressure, alongside each other, searching for a solution to the problem which arose because of the sudden awakening of the owner of the house.

This is exactly what is happening with the use of the Bible in the church! A new wind is blowing, and Christians' "memory of faith" is waking up, creating disorder in an order which was bad. The people are beginning to show us our mistakes and limitations, our unjustified usurpations.

SHIP OFF COURSE

The exegesis we were taught, the exegesis which is still being propagated even today in many books, is like a great transatlantic liner. As it crosses the sea toward its destination, it seeks to give passengers maximum safety. Size, stability, engineering, perfect service, exact information at the right time. Everything works!

But this internal safety of the ship depends on a series of external factors beyond the crew's control. It depends, for example, on the geographical map used by the captain and on the stability of the earth which guarantees the accuracy of the compass. It depends on the position of the stars and many other imponderable factors. In general the members of the crew do not think about any of this, nor do they need to.

But a slight irregularity in one of these factors may divert the ship on to an uncertain course. If that happens, all the devices designed to create safety for the passengers are put at the service of guiding the vessel toward an uncertain destination, without the crew's noticing. While looking after the internal safety of the ship, they are in fact collaborating in general insecurity. The ship's instruments were not made to detect such irregularities. They depend on regularity.

Now an irregularity of this sort will make itself felt, and the uncertain destination will start to disturb the internal safety, only when, for example, the expected port does not appear on the horizon at the moment calculated by the instruments. Then everyone wakes up and concludes, "We're lost. Something must be wrong!" And they start to look for the cause, in order to be able to correct the course of the ship and steer it toward the correct destination.

And this is exactly what is happening with the use of the

Bible in the church. Exegesis seems not to notice some different demands raised by the lives of ordinary people. It looks only at the *text* and pays almost no attention to the *context* and the *pre-text*, where imponderable factors are at work, different from those at work at the time of the installation of the analytic instruments which today guide scientific exegesis. As a result, exegesis runs the risk of being on course for a place where there is no port in which to dock and no people to take on board. It runs the risk of not providing the people of God with the service they expect of it.

When the Pre-text Is Missing

All three are necessary, text, pre-text, and context, each fulfilling its own function. If this is not the case, the system does not function and the word of God fails to attain its objective in people's lives. The predominance of one factor or the absence of another disrupts or makes impossible the functioning of all three.

Once a priest said to me:

> You know what I'm finding? The people take the Bible and start reading. They want to take the content seriously, but the environment in which they do their reading does not encourage them. It is a world confined to worship and religion and their own lives. It has to be opened up more, otherwise the people get completely confused and lost in an attitude very like that of the sects. We try to widen their horizons with courses on health, on union work, etc., but, as they see it, all that's so far from the Bible and faith that they do not even see that one may have something to do with the other. They want to link the Bible with life, but for want of a realistic vision this connection becomes moralistic, pietistic, and conformist.

In other words, the people read the text of the Bible, but this reading produces a closed community environment which does not allow the sun of the real world to enter with its full force. In this way the absence of a pre-text corrupts the context, with the result that the text is unable to contribute to the liberation of its readers. And not only that. The Bible text itself starts to be made absolute and mystified and confirms the people in their alienated reading, remote from the reality of life.

As the priest describes it, the people are concerned with the connection between the Bible and their lives. The people want to read the gospel in the context of real life. But when they think about "life," they do not look beyond the internal limits of the community's life. They identify the pre-text with the context. They become concerned only with the transformation of the group's life in accordance with the requirements expressed by the text of the Bible.

A community like this is no danger to the antievangelical system which governs the world and the lives of men and women. It may even reinforce it by interpreting the Bible in order to provide moral rules that conform to the external environment, without asking whether that environment is in accord with God's will or not.

CAUSES OF IGNORING THE PRE-TEXT

1. It may be *the result of the normal growth of the group.* The first result of the reading of the text is the creation and growth of a community context in which the text is read and meditated on. The text is read within the context of real life, and its connection with real life is seen, but as yet people do not look beyond the life of the group.

When this pre-text is missing, that is, when there is no perspective from the real situation in which the people live, what is also missing are the conditions necessary to enable those living in the community to discover the real meaning of the text. In this way the whole thing risks running into a dead end. It is not that the contribution of real life is rejected. No one rejects it. But it is reduced to the scale of the life lived by the group, and no one looks beyond its boundaries to the larger human community.

This narrow vision of the role of life in interpreting the Bible may have various causes, and a need is emerging to open out the reading to encompass the perspective of the larger human community of which the group is a part. It is the critical moment for opening the context to let in the pre-text which is outside the life of the community. The group may refuse to open up, because each new perspective which opens up carries with it the impression that nothing has happened so far, and that everything done so far was a waste of time. It is a moment of tensions and crises, very natural and necessary.

2. Leaving out the pre-text may be a *consequence of fear.* The problems of our world are so big that any individual despairs of being able to solve them. Especially in big cities, the conditions in which most people have to live are so overwhelming, so inhuman, and the system which maintains that situation is so strong and so all-pervading and repressive that the mere thought of having to oppose this pre-text is frightening. And the group closes ranks. It is a little like the situation of the first Christians. They had the community context of the resurrection. And on the basis of that they took on the pre-text of the world of Judaism, attempting to break with the Old Testament system, which kept them locked in a narrow view of salvation. Some didn't want to open the context to let in the outside world, the world of the pagans. They wanted to preserve the Law of Moses. St. Paul is quite clear: they were just afraid of persecution! (see Gal. 6:12). Stephen was killed when he tried to open up the context, reading the text afresh in the light of the new pre-text (see Acts 6–7).

3. Ignoring the pre-text may be *an alienated reaction to the outside world.* The group sees the evil of the system which governs the world and in which they live as outcasts, without voice or power. Their response is to create a closed environment in which they, those who have been marginalized by the system, become those who have been "saved by God in Christ." Those who live outside the community environment, outside the context, are lost and "condemned." In this way the community becomes the symbolic opposite of the real situation.

4. Finally, leaving out the pre-text may be the result of *the absence of integrated pastoral activity.* Courses on health and trade union work, such as the priest talked about, enter the community's life but are viewed as separate from the text. The people do not see them as an integral part of a single divine plan for the renewal of human life. Such pastoral activity confirms the

view which already exists, according to which life and faith are separate in practice. Pastoral work helps the two branches to grow, each in its own direction, but is unable to treat the damage at the root, the separation between the faith context and the pre-text of life.

The remedy will vary, depending on the cause which prevents the group from accepting the perspective of the wider world, but we can suggest some possible lines of action.

SOME REMEDIES

1. Humanizing the Text. To deal with the root of the problem, the separation between faith and life, the biblical text has to be presented in such a way that the people find that it "mirrors" their lives and their problems; it is necessary to insist on the "connaturality of interests and problems with the subject matter of the text" (Paul VI). There is a lot of talk about demythologizing the faith, but what seems to me much more important is bringing the content of the text into the reality of ordinary people's everyday experience, and explaining it in such a way that it is not a distant text, but a text which speaks about contemporary human life. This means more work for the exegete. She or he will have to study and attempt to get, as it were, behind the scenes of the Bible, to the human problems experienced by the people of that time. In that way people will be able to identify with the text being read and will see how the text is the product of an interaction between faith and life, between context and pre-text.

2. Strengthening the Context. It is no good just condemning a group for being closed if its members are afraid of the oppressive situation around them. They have to be strengthened so that they can overcome their fear and face the situation more confidently. They have to be able to find within themselves a power greater than that which is crushing their lives. This power can be none other than the power of the resurrection, experienced and understood in everyday things. Without this, however much discussion there is, the context will not open, and the people will remain locked within the oppressive situation and alienated from the biblical message. Because of this, small victories won by the people are very important, as are other acts and experiences that embody hope and resurrection—the realization that "unity is strength," the experience of solidarity at all levels, lived experience of the faith that "God is traveling with us," prayer, sharing, happiness, everything that brings members of a group closer together and closer to God. All this gradually strengthens the context and creates a spirit of courage to face the pre-text. It is this strengthening of the context which will help to overcome the crises of growth and open the group to take the real world seriously.

3. Never Silencing the Pre-text. Research and analysis are necessary as elements in interpreting the word of God. They are necessary to make the members of the group understand that their group life does not and cannot exist in isolation from other people, that it is impossible to repair and improve their lives without attacking the general causes of problems in the world. Also very important is the people's natural wisdom. It is a very strong peg on which to hang the message of the text and create the right context. We should never forget that the wisdom of the people of the Bible existed before Abraham and the prophets. Wisdom was the environment into which the prophetic word fell, like a stone in a still lake, creating ripples until it reached the shore.

It is not too much to say that forgetting the pre-text is one of the main reasons why the Bible does not always produce its liberative effect. This is not true just of the people, but also for research in exegesis. The call to take account of the pre-text in interpreting the text is not a dictum derived from abstract reasoning, but derives from the unity of the divine plan: the liberating word of the gospel must be grafted onto the trunk of human life brought into being by the creative Word. Creation and salvation are two volumes of the same divine book.

When the Context Is Missing

A priest said to me, "When I read or hear some interpretations of the Bible, I get the impression that people have a hidden agenda. Before starting to interpret the text, they know what they're going to find in it. They reduce the meaning of the Bible to the scale of their own ideas." And another added: "It's an ideological, tendentious, use of the Bible. In their eyes the community is no more than an action group for changing society." These two remarks, which admittedly seem somewhat exaggerated, express the importance and the need for taking the context into account in the interpretation of the Bible.

The context of the living community is, in St. Paul's phrase, "a letter from Christ. . . ,written not with ink but with the Spirit of the living God" (2 Cor. 3:3). Without this living letter there is no light to illuminate the written letter and reveal its meaning-for-us. Without the living context, all that is left is the letter. But the letter kills; it is the Spirit which gives the letter life and meaning (see 2 Cor. 3:6). What is vital in interpreting the Bible is the eye of faith, created by the Spirit who called the text into being. Without the environment of faith or without the perspective of the Spirit, there are only the two poles of the text and the pre-text.

It is not that, in this difficulty, anyone is denying the contribution of the context and of faith. No one denies it. Rather the criticism being raised is that the community, the context, is reducing the text to the scale of its own plans for social action. In such a case the community runs the risk of being turned into or regarded as a group whose sole object is to act on the pre-text of society in such a way as to change it in accordance with the demands of the gospel that the group sees expressed by the text. But can the context, that is, the faith community, be only a means, an instrument? I do not think so. It is also a foretaste of the final celebration!

That is not just a theoretical point. It is only if Christians already live the final celebration, if they make the resurrection present in ordinary life, that everyone will see "the letter that everyone can read" (2 Cor. 3:2); only then shall we find the additional element which will help us to be critical of our own plans for action.

That is why those who look only at the pre-text, the society to be transformed, and do not pay sufficient attention to the context, the community, the church, are in the long run depriving themselves of a crucial instrument in their plan for change; and the same is true of those who look at the context only insofar as it can contribute to the transformation of society. In the long run both groups may be damaging the hammer of the context they want to use to change the pre-text. In this way they may be compromising the very historical endeavor to which they are committed.

The great question today is: What is our historic endeavor, our project? Christians face a challenge: What historic project are we offering, we who criticize and never accept any of the projects proposed by others? Christians have no reply. They have no viable project. There is no so-called third way. Why? Because there is not a sufficiently strong context; there is no context of risen life to give us a practical example of what Christians are to do in history. We are still in the early days. Asking Christians to have a project of their own today is like expecting primary pupils to take a final university exam. It is impossible. The pupils are not ready. It would be wrong to be angry with the pupils and say, "You're no good at this." It would also be wrong to hand them someone else's doctoral thesis and say, "You'd do better to follow these ideas." Christians will not accept this, not because the ideas are no good, but because, for the moment, the overwhelming majority of them are not in a position to judge whether the other person's doctoral thesis suits their aspirations and their faith. The context of faith needs to be able to grow more and become stronger within the lived reality of the people's life.

All this shows that there is inevitably a constant tension between text, pre-text, and context. Each of the three must have autonomy in relation to the other two; if not, the use of the Bible may be corrupted, and it may become a means of oppressing the people.

The Demands of the Text

The text is never missing. Without it there can be no interpretation. What is sometimes missing is the autonomy the text should enjoy in relation to the context and the pre-text. When the text is subordinated to the interests of the context, we get a dogmatic and apologetic exegesis. When it is subordinated to the interests of the pre-text, we may get an ideological exegesis.

It is difficult to avoid all these dangers, and they can never be completely avoided, for we all read the text from a particular perspective. The important thing is to remain aware of these dangers and to allow for the fact that one's own starting-point is only one among others.

The specific work of studying the text can be described as "giving full weight to the rights of the written text in a face-to-face conversation with the Word." We must constantly be on guard against distorting the text in order to support our own ideas. Every reading of the Bible in search of a meaning-for-us must be constantly criticized to make sure that this meaning-for-us is really rooted in the text of the Bible, in its meaning-in-itself.

On the other hand, the text requires that it be read within the context of faith, since it is the perspective of the Spirit which gives us the light to see the meaning of the text for life today. It also has to be read in the light of the pre-text, the reality of ordinary people's lives, because it is the perspective of real life which shows the full historical dimension of the conversion which the text and the Spirit are asking of us.

The rediscovery of the context is making people get together in informal groups to read the text. The rediscovery of the pre-text is making people feel the need of a more critical and judicious use of the "text."

The absence of the pre-text leads people to get trapped in a religious ghetto. The lack of the context leads people to lose their sensitivity to the presence of the living Christ among them. Now, if that sensitivity is lost, we are left with the word alone, without its master and source. We lose the freedom to interpret the word, and the word is mystified as the supreme and rigid authority. We reach a situation in which the people are "conquered by the letter of the Bible but not captured by its message." The letter becomes dead.

THE REPERCUSSIONS OF POPULAR EXEGESIS

People ask us for bread and we offer them a handful of theories about each verse of John 6 [the exegete L. Alonso Schöckel].

The priests are not very sure about the reality of a base church. The presbyters are still very insecure, frightened of losing their positions, their buildings, their comforts.

Repercussions on Exegetes

Popular interpretation of the Bible is beginning to inconvenience exegetes. Once a North American exegete, a university professor, came through Brazil. He said to me, "You exegetes in Brazil ought to write more academic articles in European journals." I replied, "I know that what you write about the Bible in academic journals is useful and necessary. But I have a very big problem about seeing how such difficult and complicated arguments meet the practical needs we feel here. When I'm explaining them to others, sometimes I just dry up, because I see that our people aren't in a position to understand anything of exegetical studies in the form in which they are usually presented. They do not help them to solve their problems of life and faith." The exegete did not like this much, and looked at me incredulously. To him that sounded like heresy.

A few days later we went to visit a colleague who lives in a very poor district of a hill town near the sea. As we went through the area and got a close-up view of the people's lives, the North American suddenly stopped. All he said was, "What I teach back home can't be applied here in the way I teach it. You have to keep on looking for the answer which I don't know."

This incident illustrates what is going on in the heads of many exegetes and priests. Trained to be the interpreters of the Bible to the people, and wanting to carry out this mission, they are keenly aware of the gulf which exists between their biblical scholarship and the practical demands of our people's life and faith. The people are not scholars. "We don't know about books," said a woman from Acre. "We just have our faith and our courage!" Dazzled by other people's knowledge, people get an inferiority complex about their ignorance, keep quiet and say, "You talk, Father. Who are we? You're educated, Father." Their dependency is increased. They do not grow.

Exegetes who are used to debating complex problems with academics and who are then confronted with the problems of

popular interpretation are at a loss and say, "You carry on looking for the answer that I don't know." They are like the psy-
chologist with her doctorate in child psychology who had to learn
from her maid how to suckle her first child. When her first child
was born she discovered that "theory is different than practice."
That was when her post-graduate studies in child psychology
really began.

A painful soul-searching has started among exegetes about
their mission in the church today. One of them writes: "We've
been so peaceful in our biblical scholarship that we've lost our
sense of its limitations and the freedom to submit it to criticism.
A huge load of knowledge, mainly knowledge about hypotheses,
has been piled up on every square meter of the biblical text,
turning it into something distant, difficult, almost unintelligible."
He goes on, "People ask us for bread and we offer them a
handful of theories about each verse of John 6. They ask questions about God and we offer them three theories about the
literary form of one Psalm. They thirst for justice, and we offer
them a discussion about the root of the word *sedaga* ('justice' in
Hebrew). I am examining my conscience out loud, and the reply
I hear is: the one must be done without neglecting the other"
(L. Alonso Schöckel, professor at the Biblical Institute in
Rome). In another article, published in *Concilium*, the same
exegete asks, "Do the Christians of Latin America need North
American specialists for the word of God to speak to them?
How far do the more or less Catholic peoples of the Mediter-
ranean need the German exegetical miracle?"

Exegetes are beginning to show unmistakable signs of loss of
identity and insecurity about their mission in the church. They
feel like the man who has studied and knows all the properties
of salt but is a bad cook. The food turns out with a strange taste,
and the people it was prepared for do not like it. The people,
for their part, who know little or nothing about the properties
of salt, have started to use it without asking the exegete's per-
mission, and despite the simplicity of their cookery, they have
turned out to be good cooks. We can say, then, that the practice
of Christians, ambivalent though it may be, reveals some of the
limitations of current exegesis, provides a critique of the way
exegesis uses scholarship, and is provoking a wholesale self-

questioning among exegetes. Once submerged in day-to-day pastoral activity, the exegetes discover that the scalpel of biblical scholarship does not always reach, let alone cure, the source of the problems in popular interpretation. Reality disarms them and makes them more humble, which is a good thing.

Challenges to Interpreters of the Bible

THE STARTING-POINT FOR EXEGETICAL INVESTIGATION

In a small hamlet a group met to reflect on the text which begins with the words: "There were many widows in Israel in Elijah's day." The group leader, the only person in the group who could read, read the text, making a great effort with each word. He asked if everyone had understood. No one had understood anything. "OK, I'll read it again." At the end of the second reading he asked, "Did you understand that time?" He got the same negative reply. "All right, I'll take it sentence by sentence." He read the first sentence. "There were many widows in Israel in Elijah's day." "What did you understand?" "Widows," was the reply. "All right," said the group leader, "we'll talk about our widows."

If it is true that the greatest theoretical problems debated by the specialists have, and should have, the tips of their roots dipping into the simplest problems of the poorest sections of the population, what are the real theoretical problems for us here in Brazil? If exegetes really want to serve the church in the country in which they live, what should be their theoretical problems? It is a very serious question. Are the problems confronting exegetes in Brazil the same problems as those which concern European and North American exegetes?

THE MOST IMPORTANT PROBLEMS

The people need an interpreter, a mediator, to avoid a repetition of the historic disaster which fragmented the use of the Bible in the church. In the past, for want of a clear sense of direction and a critical method, spiritual exegesis wandered off into fantasy and what is known as fideism. This did enormous damage to biblical interpretation. The people, in whom the Holy Spirit acts, were marginalized in the renewal of biblical studies which took place in the last two hundred years, and as a result the renewed biblical exegesis itself was deprived of the light which illuminates and gives meaning to the texts of the Bible. The result was the paralysis I mentioned earlier. But the people have taken up the Bible again and are now questioning the exegetes. Popular interpretation has many defects and ambivalences. How will the exegetes react? In the same way as they did two hundred years ago?

The central problem of the use of the Bible in the church has shifted from the study of the text to the contribution of the context of the community's faith and that of the pre-text of real life. The people are already practicing this integration of text, context, and pre-text. They are integrating faith, common sense, and life. But they face many difficulties which threaten to make this new development miscarry. More attention needs to be paid to this as a matter of urgency. And important new questions must be studied and answered. For example: How should the text of the Bible be read in relation to a social situation that is being presented and evaluated by scientific criteria different from those we are used to? We say that the Bible is being read within the context of the community's faith. But what exactly does "context of faith" mean? Is it the local or regional community? Is it the diocese? These are new problems, which are not in the textbooks, but the way ahead depends on solving them.

HAVING THE RIGHT ATTITUDE

If the Bible's aim is that the people should be able to find a meaning for their lives and struggles, then exegetes have to look for the criteria of their academic investigations in terms of that aim. If a car is intended to run on dirt roads, the manufacturer must take that into account from the first moment of production. It is no good saying, "That's the drivers' problem. Let them deal with it." Taking that attitude would result in many disasters and the manufacturer would go out of business. If the Bible exists to be made relevant to life, exegetes, even if their function is to work out the literal and historical meaning, cannot say, "Making the Bible relevant isn't my business. It's a matter for parish priests and pastoral workers. Let them deal with it!" The aim of the Bible must shape the attitude and the approach of every activity that has to do with the Bible. If this emphasis were really present in all works of exegesis, even the driest and most remote from everyday life, the results of these investigations (the ten thousand articles and books a year) would be doing much more toward solving pastoral problems.

Repercussions on Priests and Pastors

For many priests this way of interpreting the Bible is so different that, even with the best will in the world, they are unable to understand and still less able to take part in and help the growth of this new movement. "The priests are not very sure about the reality of a base church." Sometimes the reason is not just insecurity, but the fear of "losing their positions, their buildings, their comforts."

But there is no reason for so much anxiety. Priests and pastors should find comfort in the fact that the anonymous voice of the people has found spokesmen in the popes themselves. For instance, in an address to the twenty-first Italian Bible Week, Paul VI went further than many exegetes and priests. His address — which I have already cited extensively but which has added meaning in the context of the present topic — was important in outlining what is expected today of biblical interpreters working with the people. The pope said:

Fidelity to the Incarnate Word also requires, in virtue of the dynamic of the incarnation, that the message be made present, in its entirety, not to people in general, but to the men and women of today, those to whom the message is now being proclaimed. Christ became the contemporary of a particular group of people and spoke their language. *Fidelity to him requires that this contemporaneity continue.* This is the whole mission of the church, with its tradition, its magisterium and its preaching. Exegetes must contribute to this task. Fidelity to the people of today is difficult and demands effort, but it is necessary if we are to remain totally faithful to the message. Between the two fidelities, fidelity to the Incarnate Word and to the people of today, there cannot and must not be opposition [in *Acta Aposto-licae Sedis* 62 (1970), pp. 615–18].

In other words, there cannot and must not be opposition between the meaning-in-itself which exegesis seeks and the meaning-for-us which the people seek.

In the same address the pope makes a distinction between exegesis and hermeneutics (interpretation). He defines exegesis as a "traditional activity" concerned with the scientific study of the text; it includes textual criticism, historical criticism, and literary criticism. But the interpretation of the Bible cannot be reduced to the work of exegesis, as it tended to be a little while ago. The more important problems we have to face no longer fall under the heading "exegesis," but under that of "herme-neutics." Hermeneutics has to do with the work required to discover the meaning of the text for us today and to integrate this meaning into our lives. The pope highlights three particular problems connected with hermeneutics:

1. Interpretation will not have exhausted its task until it has demonstrated how the meaning of scripture can refer to the present moment of salvation, that is, when it has shown its application to the present circumstances of the church and the world. . . .

2. The person of the interpreter is not detached from the process of interpretation, but is involved in it. The interpreter's whole being is called in question.

3. It is necessary to look for a certain connaturality of interests and problems with the subject matter of the text, if we are to be open to it and able to hear it.

In more difficult words, the pope was saying the same thing as the people when they start to read the Bible. The following quotations from the reports on the base communities highlight this:

1. "We just want to know what the text has to say about how we should live."

2. "We meet around the gospel to understand it; why not make the effort to put it into practice?"

3. "Since we've been learning to read the Bible, we've begun to find real life in it." It is "a mirror of life."

With Vatican Council II, one era ended and another began. It was the end of the era of almost exclusive preoccupation with the meaning of the text-in-itself. However, the church documents which still shape the attitudes of many priests and bishops with regard to the interpretation of the Bible are almost all from the period between Vatican I and Vatican II. Paul VI, in the address I have just quoted, refers to the encyclical *Divino Afflante Spiritu* and to chapters 3 and 6 of the Vatican II constitution, *Dei Verbum*. He relativizes both the encyclical and the two chapters, saying that they are concerned with "exegesis" understood as the "traditional activity" concerned with the text of the Bible. But the problem today is different. It is no longer a matter of defending the root, the "letter" of the Bible; the time has come to present the fruit produced from the root, that is, the meaning of the text for people's lives.

"A Tool Which Extracts the Content"

What content? Memory does not preserve the past as something over and done with but as a living and active force which pushes the present toward the future. The real past has not stayed in the past. It is part of the foundations of the future; it lies behind the eyes today looking toward the future. When we drink from the spring of revelation, it is not as though its water has flowed all along a subterranean bed of history until it finally burst forth at our tap in the present. Rather the spring has accompanied the people throughout their journey, like the "spiritual rock" in the desert (1 Cor. 10:4), and wells up from within us, from the sense the people have of being the people of God. And this water is welling up today, clear and sparkling, among the people. Through the use they make of the Bible, the memory of faith is awakening and a new vision of both the Bible and life is looking for a way through to the surface of consciousness. What is this vision? What is its content? We may get closer to answering these questions by expanding upon and further focusing on two analogies I referred to in a different context in an earlier chapter.

This ancient and yet vitally new vision I am trying to describe can be summed up in the image St. Augustine invented. God wrote two books. The first book is not the Bible, but creation, life, history, facts, the whole reality of human life, everything human beings do and produce for their well-being, the meaning-in-itself of things, the "letter," as the Fathers of the church used to say, all that touches us closely, the pre-text. But this first book became totally opaque and lost its clarity. Its letters faded as a result of human sin. It no longer spoke of God. It no longer revealed its meaning, except "with much difficulty and lengthy effort by our minds."

Because of this God wrote another book:

The Holy Spirit, the finger of God, which had already writ-ten the letters of the creation, set to work to compose this new book and spread over us the sky of the scriptures. It is like a new firmament, which, like the first, tells forth the power of God and, more than the first, sings of his mercy. Thanks to it, the faculty of contemplation was restored to us and so all creation becomes for us a revelation of God.

This means that the second book, the Bible, is not an end in itself. It exists in function of the first book, in function of life and human history. This life of ours is "opaque," damaged, op-pressed, no longer flowers. And we cannot see this damage. It was to enable us to rediscover the meaning of life and history, to enable us to rediscover what God wants of us, and to guide us in putting human life to rights, that we were given the Bible.

"Scripture explains what creation puts before us," the Fath-ers used to say. It is as in an art exhibition, where the visitor gets a catalogue which explains the meaning of the works on show. *The Bible is the catalogue of the world,* which Christians receive from its creator to enable them to understand the mean-ing of the various elements of life and to discover the meaning they have to give to the parts which need repair. An exhibition without a catalogue confuses visitors, while a catalogue without an exhibition is nonsense. This shows the futility of an exclusive insistence on the Bible, as though it alone could bring salvation.

This is the vision which is awakening among the people.

Where it is able to grow, it functions like a seed which has as its ultimate fruit the resurrection, the full unfolding of life, just as God imagined it on the day of creation.

The vision which is extracted by the tool of the people's method, therefore, is the vision of a world to be transformed, of a new life to be generated, of a hope to be fulfilled, of a human race to be re-created.

The true content or synthesis of things is not the one the exegete or theologian sketches out on paper to be implemented subsequently. Rather this true content or synthesis is uncovered haltingly and painstakingly in the midst of life and is therefore always subject to "re-reading" and correction. It is never revealed perfectly and absolutely in our lives, but it is still necessary that we work to implement it as a historical project that will enable the historical process to move on and progress. It is necessary as a "tutor to lead to Christ," as a stage, scaffolding, a lift for part of the journey. The real and perfect synthesis, the real content, comes from God and is already imprinted on life and history, and has been since the creation. It is not something to be venerated but to be developed and fulfilled in history by human beings. We come close to this synthesis, step by step, with our syntheses and projects, which are constantly "re-read" and corrected. As I said before, today we are in a phase of re-reading. With the help of the elements we find in the world and society as they develop, and especially in the people in which the creator's project is awakening, we are able to criticize the previous syntheses and gradually formulate the draft of a new synthesis which takes us a little nearer to the goal God has fixed for humankind.

This is the "theory" which arises out of "practice" and begins slowly to develop, taking shape in the people's initiatives.

Repercussions on the System

All these remarks, incidents, and attitudes in the people's dealings with the Bible reveal a new mentality. A new wind is blowing, signaling an imminent change in the weather. It is creating insecurity among those who feel at home only in the previous system, but is welcomed by those who were already worrying about the drought and beginning to think that it would never rain again.

The people are beginning to live, act, and talk no longer out of knowledge they have received, but out of a knowledge they have discovered for themselves. They no longer accept teachers who distribute ideas and formulas, but want a fellow student who will discuss problems with them on an equal footing.

They are beginning to live, act, and talk no longer in terms of values received from others like alms, but out of life which is springing up from within themselves. The experience and the practice of these new values are forcing some of those who had privileged power and knowledge to abandon their privileges and begin to see power and knowledge as service.

The people are beginning to live, act, and talk out of a new and mighty power, which they have discovered within themselves, in their unity with each other and with God. They are discovering that they are capable of doing great things. As a report from one community stated: "This work is creating greater unity here and elsewhere. Today we see that it's possible to do something; we've lost our fear. We're learning to defend ourselves in dealings with others. We don't know how it happens, but we do so much without knowing anything. You can feel the power of the Holy Spirit."

The people are beginning to speak with authority, "appealing to the authority of the gospel," and are no longer simply accepting any decree from an authority. They will accept it only when it is in agreement with and can be justified by the gospel and by life.

This new mentality is, for the moment, just a flower, weak and unprotected. It grows slowly. But it is a proof that it is possible and practicable to implement God's plans for the future of humankind. That is why, despite being weak and defenseless, it is already creating problems for those in the world and in the church who want to be holders of knowledge and power. "The world is growing afraid of you, defenseless flower."

It is worthwhile watering this plant, giving it fertilizer, letting the sun get to it, because it is not just an idea, but a force, a historical force stronger than us, in which we can see the effect in history of the power of the resurrection.

In the end, we can say that this force is the origin of the new ideas the people are proclaiming today as they make the Bible their own. These ideas are precursors of the new reality which is about to be born. The people have detected and articulated what is gestating. That is why their ideas are so penetrating. They are like John the Baptist who prepared the way. But, when Christ finally came, he did not behave as John had proclaimed he would. John was uncertain: "Are you the one who is to come, or are we to expect someone else?" (Mt. 11:3). Jesus told John first to compare the vision of the future John had proclaimed with the future which was arriving in the person and work of Jesus and then to correct his ideas about the future: "Go back and tell John what you hear and see" (Mt. 11:4).

This may happen—it certainly will happen—to the John the Baptists who are today trying to prepare the way for God's future. About the future, for the moment, we have only ideas and theories, but the future is greater than the ideas and theories which proclaim it and bring it to pass. This is the problem with theories and systems: they get locked inside a limited range of ideas. Forged to be vehicles of life, they end up choking that life and forcing it to fit into their own limited scope of ideas. But in the end life breaks the rope that is strangling it and rises again.

TOWARD A LIBERATING EDUCATION: SOME QUESTIONS

I speak in twisted words. I describe my life without understanding it.

You must bear with my silly questions when I talk. It's ignorance. I don't talk to any outsiders, hardly. I can't put things properly. I did learn a little with my buddy Quelemém, but he wants to know everything differently; he does not want the matter on its own, clear, but the thing underneath, the other thing [J. Guimaraes Rosa, in Grande Sertão: Veredas*].*

How Do You Express the Real Word in Real Life?

This was exactly the question raised by a group of animators who work in the basic ecclesial communities. Throughout the meeting I felt that the two women from the parish team were not very happy with the theme as I was presenting it. I was talking almost entirely about the Bible. Later they confirmed that my intuition had been right. They tried a number of times to lead the discussion into very practical matters of justice, wages, health, the everyday struggle, and so on. This is where I begin to wonder about the right way to express the word of God in the context of real life.

I did not make any explicit connections between the Bible and those practical matters, and did not want to at that point. I do not know which of us was right, I or they. I tried to work out why I was resisting them like that, and I offered the following explanation:

> It does not help much to bend two branches of the same tree to bring their tips nice and close. This closeness will only last as long as you hold the two branches. As soon as you let them go, each branch will go back to its original position and everything will be as it was before. My idea is this: the two branches, although separated from each other in the space of life, are already united at the trunk and above all at the root and the earth. I try to enable the people simply to descend along the branch of the word of God until they discover for themselves, not from me, that the word of the Bible and the word of life both spring from the same trunk and from the same root. I'm not in a hurry, nor am I very anxious to make direct, explicit connections, which are often artificial. I try to perch on the "religious" branch (which we hope merges both the word of God and the word of life), and when people ask me about the branch of the word of God, I try to focus mostly on it and thereby help them move down it toward where it meets the branch of the word of life.

How do I do that? There are three principles I try to follow: (1) When discussing a biblical topic I try to use simple and direct language, taken from experience; that sort of language brings the topic closer to life and real problems. (2) I try to discover the human problem affecting the people or the person described in the biblical text (this is the "connaturality of interests and problems" Paul VI talked about). This turns the text into a mirror of life and enables people to see themselves in it. (3) I try to keep an overall vision and to talk about the "religious" branch on the basis of this unified vision.

I remember that for me, too, my teachers' words did not always succeed in helping me discover everything they talked so passionately about. If, instead of talking to me so much *about* those things, they had talked to me *out of their experience of them;* if, instead of trying so hard to inculcate those ideas into me (ideas which were beyond my world and my reach and which I could not understand because I had nothing in my experience to relate them to); if, instead of that, they had opened doors in the dark room in which I was stuck — then I would have got the point of what they were trying to teach much sooner. The clarity of logic is not enough to persuade people of a thing and make them see its meaning for *their* life. Seeing a meaning has to do with feeling and experience, with conviction.

Stork or Midwife?

The mythic stork *presents* the child to the parents — as if the child came from outside the parents, as if there is no need for gestation and painful birth. The midwife helps in the painful birthing of the child who has been gestating in the mother's womb, and the experienced and skilled midwife knows when to intervene in the birth and when, in the best of circumstances, to stand back and let the birth occur with little intervention. Should pastoral workers function like the stork, bringing the ready-made biblical message and answers to all questions to the people, or should they function as midwives, acting only when necessary to assist the people in bringing forth the biblical message from their midst? The answer, obviously, is that pastoral workers should function more like the skilled midwife, knowing when to intervene and when not to intervene; however, functioning in that way is no simple matter.

Earlier in this book I mentioned the questions the people ask about the Bible. Perhaps in the past when I have answered these questions I have made the mistake of talking too much. I do not know if I was a stork or a midwife. Maybe I was too storklike, but then there *are* things which have to be taught, answers that have to be given. For example, faced with the question, "Who is the Levite?," does it do any good to ask, "What do you think?" and waste time, only to have to give the right answer in the end? Does that turn the discussion into a television quiz, stressing the people's ignorance, when the expert gives the right answer after everyone's gotten it wrong?

It is tempting to think that the key is for us pastoral workers to talk as little as possible so that the people can talk as much as possible. I do not think that is the heart of the problem. The problem is for us to discover our place, our mission, and our practical contribution in this great machine which is building the new world, in which we too are just one of many parts.

When the members of a Bible study group know something, they say so quite naturally. When it comes to matters involving the Bible, I try to take part in the group like one of them: if I know something I say so and speak quite naturally. Generally I do not know what to say and keep quiet, especially when we are talking about practical things like wages, laws, the land, seeds, unions, health, and so on. I do not know much about these things, and when it comes to discussing those matters I do not attempt to take part in the group just like the others. I cannot, partly because of my different culture, and partly because of the role the others cast me in—"Father."

The nub of the problem is being clear about the role of the pastoral worker in this whole process. The question of if and when a pastoral worker should intervene to assist in the birth of the biblical message from the people can be resolved only after the pastoral worker has found his or her place and has been accepted by the others. At root, it is a problem of identity, of culture, of social class. If you are of the same class as the people to whom you are talking, there is less danger of imposing outside ideas because the people answer back straightaway and will not accept such imposition.

My feeling is that we pastoral workers still have not really found our place, our necessary contribution, and therefore we can err simultaneously by nonintervention and by intervention. One sort of silence can be even more dominating than talking, and does that make for liberating education?

Finally, we need to remember that there is no such thing as spontaneous generation. The child comes from the mother and the father, and those who wish to assist in the birth of a strong child who will grow in harmony with the parents must listen to and work with the parents throughout the long period of gestation. In other words, we as pastoral workers have to listen to and be with the people in all aspects of their lives and in the long period during which the biblical message gestates in their midst. In the end maybe all we can say is that the pastoral worker should simply work to foster life. Sometimes that involves intervening, answering questions; at other times it is best to allow the biblical message to come to life on its own among the people. The goal of all this is that the "liberating word" of the gospel unite with the "creative word" which acts in life. This union results in pregnancy: within the people there grows the embryo of a new life which will one day come into the world. The people do not always need the intervention of midwives. What they need is the word which implants in them a new consciousness, a new life, new light, and new strength.

How will all this influence our educational methods and make them really liberating? That is the ultimate question.

How Is Our Language a Problem?

Once I was with a peasant and his wife in their living room. He was reading the Bible; she was reading a parish newsletter; and I was busy with something. The couple were both reading aloud, but just to themselves. Two young women from the parish team came in. One of them brought Raimundo—that was the man's name—a copy of *The Cry of the Northeast,* a magazine.

Raimundo broke off his reading of the word of God to pay attention to *The Cry of the Northeast,* and asked the young woman to read "a little bit of that lovely magazine, any bit, the bit you were reading most recently." The reading was about the history of slavery in the ancient Roman empire, as far as I remember. There were phrases like "social, economic, and political equality," "servocratic state," and "gens."

The peasant kept interrupting the reading and asking the

meaning of these words, which he could not even pronounce. I thought to myself: the academic language developed by the analysts of the world is not understood by the world they are analyzing! The language a person uses is much more than a set of words; it represents a vision of the world.

Raimundo's vision of the world is different from that of the author of the article and different from mine. I do not know exactly what Raimundo's vision is. He talks only in parables and images. He has a sense of humor which somehow puts in its place everything we "educated" pastoral workers do and say. He seems to feel and see that he and his people are the peg on which our ideas, words, and actions have to be hung. Without this peg the ideas, words, and actions will not hold up and are useless. Without him and his people our lives and activity would have no meaning.

While he may seem weak and may be ignorant about a lot of things, Raimundo, in this attitude of his, which may be unconscious, is stronger and wiser than we. He is humble, deeply humble, but at the same time full of dignity, conscious of his worth. He does not understand our language. He does not know the meaning of "social, economic, and political equality." Nevertheless, his ignorance does not make him weak. He carries on calmly. He seems to sense that our ideas have a future only when they are understood and put into practice by him and his people. He is not in a hurry. He does not worry about trying to understand everything we say. He lives at the rhythm of his people. Instead of trying to rush the people, he seems to want to put a brake on us, so that we fall into step with the people.

After all this discussion had finished, he went back to reading the word of God! He had listened to *The Cry of the Northeast,* and had made audible a different, very discreet, cry, and now was returning to feed on the word of God which supplies the life for all other words. People like that are more important than we think. He, in his simplicity and deep faith, is a sign and a spokesman for the people, in their own style. He has been imprisoned, and was not shaken. He continues to listen to "The Cry of the People" and tries to respond, guided by the word of God. But he responds in his own way.

The problem of language is much more serious than people

think. Language can be a means of communication or a barrier to communication. Words are like plants: they grow from seeds thrown on the soil. There is soil which will not produce coffee, even if you throw coffee seeds on it. The same corn grows one way in one soil and another way in another soil. One type of language, even if sown among the people, produces nothing; the soil will not produce. Rural people know the soil. Do we who are "educated" know that soil well enough to know which words will take root in it and eventually bear fruit? The only thing that will teach us this is contact, long human contact. Thirty years of human contact in Nazareth for only three years of talking! And three years enough to get Jesus killed!

Much of the language that you and I use did not originate among the people. As a result the vision it expresses and the concepts it uses are not easily assimilated by the people. We must immediately begin to listen to and try to capture the way the people express themselves and the words they use to talk about matters of faith. We shall probably rediscover in a new way old ideas which we thought we knew perfectly well already.

The reports from the basic ecclesial communities are full of the people's expressions. Here are just a few: "Once we had the freedom of the land. God gave it to us. Now human beings have robbed us of our sense of God and of ourselves. We are oppressed. We live in captivity; we are slaves, because we're dominated by the 'great.' We have to fight, get together and become strong to see if we can free ourselves. We are equal. No one is greater than another." "The most important thing is that people believe in themselves; we were born poor and we will grow only if we believe in ourselves and in others." "The good thing about this movement is that we feel ourselves people among people." Those within the church are beginning to "exchange ideas so as to discover the Holy Spirit's idea among the people." This last remark, worthy of a Church Father or a Doctor of the Church, came from a retired commercial traveler who hardly knows how to read and who does not even have electricity in his house.

The good thing about all this is that the people, in this way, are making us rediscover our ignorance. We once thought ignorance was the exclusive privilege of the "ignorant" people, but we were wrong. Through this process the "liberators" lose some of their pretensions and begin to see that they too have to be liberated from quite a few things. And we have the paradox of the would-be liberators liberated by those to whom they thought they were bringing liberation! Liberation is not a one-way street, from us to the people; rather it is a two-way street. If we find ourselves traveling on a one-way street, then there is something wrong with the method we are using.

Is the Bible Really the People's Book?

Adelaide, a member of one of the basic communities, said, "I don't know anything about all this and so I keep quiet." Leonarda said, "I'm the same. I don't know anything." Genésio said with a smile, "I stay here in my corner, just listening." Margarida just shook her head, laughing, without saying anything. Fabiano remembered something and ended: "We must love one another." Totônia had no ideas at all. That was all. No one remembered anything. No one could say anything about the parable of the sower which had been read at the beginning of the meeting. Why was this?

It is difficult to give an answer. A lot depends on the methodology and the attitude, which were probably wrong. Indeed, when the discussion went back to the jobs each person was doing in the community, everyone spoke and took an active part as though it was the most natural thing in the world. But is getting the people engaged with the Bible only a matter of method and attitude?

Where the Bible is concerned, the people profess ignorance and lack of education. Where does this ignorance come from, and how can it be removed? Through courses and training programs? Possibly, but we have to bear in mind another fact. Most diocesan training courses and classes on the Bible do indeed help to increase the people's knowledge about the Bible, but they also increase the people's complex about their ignorance of the Bible. The people's knowledge, however much it increases, continues to be a "received" and not a "discovered" knowledge. Do courses of this sort work well with an education for liberation? Many dioceses are now trying to find a type of course and training which will help the people, without increasing their feelings of dependence about other people's knowledge.

Perhaps we have learned too much in our lives and so carry around with us a set of worries and problems which may be real for us, but are artificial for the people. There is a cultural problem. Perhaps because of this the Bible was locked away in a room, separated from the people. We have managed to open only one door into this room, the one we have learned about, the door of knowledge about the content of the Bible. Unwittingly, we have forced the people to go in by this door, because at the moment there is no other. The people resist and keep a distance: "I stay here in my corner, just listening." He will go through that door only if he is dragged. It has always been like that.

But in that room there are three other blind walls in which three other doors could be cut. Maybe the people will cut these other doors, and we will abandon the first door and use only the other three, which we do not know much about as yet. Then we will be rid of our sense of the importance of our knowledge and the people will be rid of their professed ignorance. Please God!

The Water or the Fish: Which Is the More Important?

"That God may give us all his peace, let us pray to the Lord." That was the only thing the woman said during the whole two hours of the meeting. The people of the area had talked about a whole range of topics: the local dispensary, the people's involvement, the price of an injection, the death of a young woman in childbirth for lack of prompt medical attention, the right of all to life, the Bible's ban on consuming blood and pork. In short, the people were discussing details of their daily struggle and of the everyday life depicted in the Bible. And she stayed there, in her seat, just watching, quietly. She was very black, wrinkled, poor, an ordinary woman, anonymous — no one even mentioned her name. One of the many thousands and millions who fill Brazil, bearing children and caring for them, and so securing the future.

She and all the others like her are what might be called the infrastructure of society and humankind. They are the sources of faith, hope, and love. If she did not have that faith, that hope, and that selfless love, she would not bear her children and all our futures would have been cut short a long time ago. I thought of my mother, who was also like that. They are very fragile creatures, because anyone is more learned and stronger than they. They are extremely strong creatures, because no one can make such a contribution to the future as they do, by bearing and bringing up children, to whom they pass on their hope, their love, their faith in life, and their huge desire to improve the lives of the people.

The meeting was very good. The net of the discussion caught many fine fish: a sense of participation, a desire of the people to demand their rights, a desire to come together and organize, and a longing to act upon these feelings from a starting-point in God. Almost all of them took part in the discussion, except this woman. She simply said, "That God may give us all his peace, let us pray to the Lord."

At the time I hardly paid attention to what the woman said. All I saw was the fine fish we had caught between us. Now, though, that woman sticks in my memory. Why? It is the same with the face of an elderly woman I noticed among many others, watching a play put on by young people in the interior of Ceará. Two pairs of eyes, intent, just looking, with a joy coming from inside them. Now I am torn between the fish in the net and the woman who did not say anything and the other who just looked.

And then, almost without my thinking about it, this idea came to me, a simile. The two silent women and all the others like them are like the waters of the sea and the rivers which have made it possible for the fish to be born, live, and multiply until the day of our meeting, in which we threw out the net which brought such an abundant catch. Without this deep and silent water, no fish would be living, and no action of ours would be possible. This water is the great strength which created our meeting and gave such good results. All that we do, all of us, with all that we are and plan—everything is a child of this mother. It is she, through her turbulent but persistent life, who raises the problems which explode in our heads. She produces the food which enables the fish to appear and multiply. The fish is not the master or the father; it is a child. Even this interecclesial meeting of ours is a fish produced by the water!

I went in and out of the meeting, admiring the beauty of the fish. But now I am torn between the fish and the water: how can this dark, silent water produce such shining fish? And how are we to look after the water? Nowadays even the seas are dying because of pollution. The water would seem to have no way of defending itself against the pollution. Many rivers have already died and no longer have fish in them. The people would seem to have no defense against the propaganda of the system which pollutes everything! Rivers of dead thoughts are poured out every day into the sea of life! What will happen, what will we do, if the water is completely polluted?

I puzzle over these questions but then remember a remark by Pablo Neruda, which goes more or less like this: "The lives of the people of the land are not being corrupted, and won't be corrupted, even when surrounded by the greatest corruptions." I think he was right. But I agree without knowing why. Perhaps because I believe that life is stronger than death. When Christ died, everything seemed polluted, threatened with death, without a future. But life rose again! In the last analysis it is faith in the resurrection which makes us believe in the regenerating and liberating power of these weak people, seemingly helpless against the system which crushes, pollutes, kills, and oppresses them.

The Fish's Greatest Temptation?

An Indian sage once said, "If a fish were to study, the last thing it would discover would be the water in which it lives!" It seems to me that this is the great problem of many people who design plans for the liberation of the people—they are not sufficiently aware that they and their plans are children of the people. They are like fish who are unaware of the water. They want to be the masters of the mother who gave them birth and who sustains them.

The fish feels this temptation of power because when it pushes against the water, the water immediately yields and seems to have no contrary reaction. You can do what you like with it. It obeys. Likewise, those who think they are liberators of the people make pronouncements about their plans for the people's liberation, and the people offer no resistance. The "liberators" get a sense of power, and may come to believe they can move out of the midst of the people and then from a distance better contemplate and guide the people's movements. Illusion! Pure illusion! These "liberators" and their plans become like fish out of water—that is, short-lived. They cut themselves off from the very body that gave them life and sustenance. But the sea continues and keeps on producing those who long to be liberators. They, almost all of them, have succumbed to this great temptation and have tried to be the masters and parents of the people who gave them birth! But they have all been defeated, swept from the face of the earth by the violence of the waters they thought they controlled as lords and masters! And the people continue on their way, always being betrayed by these "children," but not despairing, producing new children and passing on to them their dream, their huge desire to be a true people, hoping to give birth one day to the one who will really liberate them and give them peace.

Why should so many liberation movements, produced by the people's situation of oppression, have produced so little result till now? Who are the real liberators of the people? It is a question that we must soon answer.

Being radical in the struggle for liberation requires that the liberator should realize that he or she is a fish produced, brought into the world and kept alive by the water, totally dependent on it, incapable of living on dry land for even five minutes. It means becoming humble like the water itself, not deluding oneself with the lack of resistance of the water, not thinking that one "has the people in the palm of one's hand." No one has the people in the palm of his or her hand. No one liberates the people unless the people liberate that person!

Jesus Christ was a true radical. He was a fish who never cut himself off from the water. In him, to this day, the people recognize and renew their acquaintance with their aspirations. He overcame the temptations of domination: bread (charity), spectacular gestures (populism), power (governing by the force of authority and knowledge).

What could the woman I mentioned earlier have meant by

peace? I do not know. Certainly she was not thinking of Bush and Gorbachev, or of armies and war, or of multinationals and economic power. I think she simply wanted to express the peace she was feeling at that moment: the peace of a closely united group of people concerned for others, wanting to serve their fellows, organizing to do that and praying to God. Perhaps she thought of her family, of their problems, and she felt the urge: "That God may give us all his peace, let us pray to the Lord." The leader's temptation is to want to be the master of the people. The people's temptation is to want to lose themselves in the happy moments they experience, not to think beyond that and forget the large movement of history. The leader's temptation arises precisely out of this desire of the people to be swayed by the leaders and try to rest complacently in moments of happiness and peace. How do we get the balance right? I have no final answer.

Through her calm presence to the end of the meeting and through her prayer, the woman approved the action of the group. And this approval is important. It is she, the water, the people, who, in the last analysis, will judge the action of the group and of its leaders. That is why all groups and leaders ought to be constantly open and sensitive to the criticism that may come from the poorest sections of the people. Many groups and communities formed some years ago should make a serious examination of conscience and see if routine and impatience are not creating a distance between them and the people. The only way for them to make this examination of conscience is to open themselves and all their activity to the criticism of the masses. Such criticism may bring surprises and be the stimulus for a new conversion. A fish cannot live out of water.

For those who want to work for the liberation of the people, contact with the people—being at close quarters with them in all their weakness and anonymity—should be what strengthens and fuels their action, purifying it constantly and keeping it in the right direction. The force that generates liberation does not rest ultimately in discussion groups, but runs through them and is firmly fixed in the heart of this anonymous and suffering people, weak and unprotected. It is from there that liberation movements must draw their strength, because it is there that the creative Word acts.

What Is the Bible for? What Is the Use of the Gospel?

We who wish to work with the people must recognize that the Bible, the gospel, and our pastoral approach are not the only forces shaping the people. This influence come also through the radio, through the new road nearby, through the market, through so many channels. The change in people's minds is already taking place, with us and without us. We notice the difference between the outlooks of the people in inner cities, outlying districts, and rural areas. These differences did not come from us; they came from the great cultural river which is invading everything today.

Who is giving the people their critical outlook? The gospel or society itself as it changes? I think in fact that our changing society is giving much more critical sense and awareness of things than the gospel is in the form we preach it. On all sides ordinary people are waking up, thinking differently from the way they thought twenty years ago. It is not the gospel which is waking them up; it is society. And our preaching, the Bible, the gospel: What use is it? Just for waking people up?

Many people are interested in waking the people up. Some use the gospel to do this. They are quite right. In this situation the gospel acts as one of many elements in a global strategy for change. It acts like one of the beacons to guide the movement of change and conversion which is flowing through the world today. The gospel is absorbed into the historical projects based on logic. This is not being unfaithful to the gospel. On the contrary, it is necessary that the gospel guide and even critique the work of logic with a view to the liberation of the people.

Even so, I feel that all this is not totally satisfying. That is not all the people expect from the gospel. It is not infidelity to the gospel, but there is one part of the gospel, one aspect, which does not get the status it should have. It is the part which has to do with feasts, novenas, pilgrimages, prayers, and celebrations—that part of the gospel which is simply useless, which cannot be used for anything, because it is no use for anything;

it is not efficient. It is the part which makes us waste time, the precious time of efficiency, and makes those who want to achieve something impatient, the part which is relaxation, entertainment, pure play. This is the part in which we acknowledge that we are small, humble, impotent, in which we simply "play before God" and delight the Father, just as a child playing delights its parents.

Doing nothing, being lazy, before God, being useless, sensing the gratuitousness of life and enjoying it, without any other purpose except the joy of living in fellowship with God and our fellows — this part of the gospel takes away from us the immense seriousness of logic and projects and restores us to our place. We Christians are not the saviors of the world. The savior of the world is Christ, son of God our Father. Knowledge of that fact helps us develop the courage to do something for liberation, because we know liberation is already guaranteed by the power of God, even if we have to die and not see any fruit throughout our lives.

This leaves some space for laughter and jokes. If it did not, seriousness would have killed us all or at least had us all in psychiatric hospitals. The Bible has parts whose only purpose is to bring a smile to the lips of the reader.

I do not know if I am right, but I suspect that when the gospel is forced to fit into logic's projects, it bursts out on the other side in the people, in pilgrimages, novenas, prayers, miraculous and divine cures, processions, Pentecostalism, and charismatic renewal. And when people try to reduce the gospel simply to prayers and feasts, logic wakes up and sweeps it away as something useless.

Is this all an intellectual's theoretical problem? I do not know. Look at it in terms of the little hamlet where I spent five days, on the borders of Piauí and Ceará. Our logic was all about pipes for water, production of maize and cassava, old age pensions, education for the children, meetings and organization. The playful dimension burst out in novenas, which were carried out with lively music and joy.

The people are able to enter into our logic and travel with us for a long time. They give us the impression that they are taking in everything we preach. They are capable of having the meetings we ask them to have and of laying pipes for water, but they do it in part so that they can have "Father" at least once a year for their great "entertainment," the open-air Mass. They will never miss a party!

Who is right, they or we? We tend to be consumed in logic and work and seek leisure only insofar as it will help us to work. They work so that one day they can have leisure, enjoy life, and feel the gratuitousness of everything that comes from God: thus having "life to the full" (Jn. 10:10).

I once heard two priests discussing the attitude of a third, who was more involved in "recreation" than in "work." He did not fit easily into the model the other two had in their heads. One said, "He needs a good drenching with conscientization!" I thought to myself, "I hope he never gets it, because then he'll stop getting on their nerves, and there'll be no one else to criticize them."

The Bible tells us two things: "Life is a struggle" and "Life is a game." Work and leisure, efficiency and uselessness, struggle and contemplation, logic and poetry, organization and charism, two branches from one and the same root, the root of life, created by God and saved in Jesus Christ. In his famous book *Homo Ludens,* written quite a number of years ago, Huizinga shows how the modern culture of consumption and efficiency is killing the dimension of life that should be given to contemplation, leisure, uselessness, poetry. Even leisure is subordinated to profit. It is a complete inversion of the natural order. This mentality also frustrates the activity of the person who works only to see some "result," who disregards anything that does not fit into the pattern of efficiency. We need both struggle and contemplation for life to develop fully and be really free.

How can we ensure that all this is really part of the educational method we adopt? That is another question I cannot answer definitively.

"The Voice of the People Is the Voice of God" —An Awkward Problem?

"The voice of the people" is not just what the people say and make explicit, but also what they do not say, what they keep quiet about. It is their whole way of being and acting, their behavior and attitudes. In a word, it is their life in all its dimensions. This life contains an inexplicable mystery which has something do with God. "The Voice of the People is the Voice of God."

THE PEOPLE'S "SILENCE"

The people have been silent for centuries. They do not reveal their thinking. For them there is no truth in the saying "Silence gives consent." The people have been instructed, the objects of teaching and propaganda. Despite this, the root seems to have been stronger than the graft. Confronted with someone who talks a lot and "knows" a great deal, the people keep quiet and maintain their reserve. The logic of the instructor's arguments is powerless before some of the people's intuitions, which logic treats as mistaken. Pilgrimages, shrines, and novenas run across the centuries, despite all efforts at "conscientization."

There is something in the people's life which cannot be reduced to intellectual concepts. Intellect keeps coming up against something which shows it its limits and invites it to be more humble, to look for a different support than its own reasoning. Intellect will be right when it succeeds in putting into words something of the mystery which exists in life and when the people (who do not know anything and do not talk) are able to recognize in its concepts something of their life.

God, too, is like that. God is not reducible to our concepts. We always run into our limitations when we try to talk about God. The challenging silence of the people is like the challenging silence of God.

THE PEOPLE'S "PATIENCE"

No one can beat the people at patience. Their capacity for resistance has run down the centuries. Dominators have been born, battled, wearied, and died. They have been defeated by this limitless resistance. It was in the same way that Christ defeated the oppressive power which crucified him. In the struggle that power exhausted all its resources and its defeat was therefore total.

This patience and resistance are attitudes of people who

know that time is on their side. They are attitudes of people
who seem weak but who are really strong. The powerful persons
who want to dominate and seemingly succeed in dominating
meet their limits here: they conquer bodies but not minds.

The people, conquered by brute force, are not won over. At
root, though crushed, they remain free. In this way they provoke
the dominators to even greater anger: they thrash around until
they fall dead from exhaustion, defeated by the people's resistance.

THE PEOPLE'S "HOPE"

The people produce their children and never tire of producing them. They may be half dead, but not even that stops them
from producing new life. They are an inexhaustible spring which
does not stop and never dries up.

The dominators organize their power in systems, construct
ideologies. In the course of the centuries systems have succeeded one another, but they have never been able to affect this
source of generation and regeneration, which continues un-
changeable, carrying and supporting even the systems which
seek to suck it dry.

This is the struggle between life and death, and life is stronger
than death. Those on the side of life have a vague awareness of
this and so are in no hurry. They have patience, for they know
God is stronger than dominators and systems.

This strange strength of the people appears all over the place,
especially where life is most under attack. The life of the poor
people preserves a disorienting vitality which reveals the limitations of "modernity."

THE PEOPLE'S "HUMANITY"

Despite all the bad things that exist in the world, the people
of the land are not being corrupted by money, by violence, by
power, by the desire for revenge, or by egoism. There is within
them a basic attitude of love.

God is not corrupted, despite the many wrong ideas about
God which corrupt the lives of many people. The people support
themselves without power, without knowledge, without possessions, and in this way show the limits and the relativity of these

things. They show that these things can have meaning only when rooted in God.

The voice of the people is the voice of God. I do not know for sure that what I have been saying in this section is right, but if the above statement is true, then I believe that what I have been saying will have a certain influence and implication in the liberating educational technique that you and I adopt.

What I mean is this. These days theology talks a lot about the "absence of God," the "silence of God." We have even heard of the "death of God" and the "grave of God." If it is true that the voice of the people is the voice of God, then where the people are not listened to, God is not listened to. Where the people are absent, God is absent too!

Could it be that this "absence of God" has something to do with the organization of the world as we know it? In the organization of power, knowledge, and wealth, the people have no say. They are merely objects. They have been marginalized. And, like the people, God has been relegated to the sidelines. God is absent, in fact, from the class which has monopolized power, knowledge, and wealth.

But since theologians in general do not belong to the marginalized class of the people, but to the class of power, money, and knowledge, they cannot talk in any other way: with their theology they ratify the dead end into which society has slipped. They give support to Christians of their own class and enable them to go on being "religious" in spite of everything. The theologians enable these people "to live in the presence of God as though God did not exist!" The theologians even spend a lot of time meditating on Jesus' words on the cross, "My God, why have you abandoned me?" They find a model in Jesus. But this saying of Jesus' is really repeated every day by the suffering people. No one believes in the presence of God more than the people.

We have to be born again, as Jesus told Nicodemus. We have to live "with our ears glued to the ground" in order to listen at close quarters to the mysterious beatings of the heart of the marginalized people, the signs of the presence of God, the true God. God is present at the "edges," where God was relegated by human beings. There God remains, with wisdom and power, challenging our power and knowledge. God went with the people into captivity and did not remain in Jerusalem when the temple was destroyed and the sacrificial fire extinguished. The temple will be rebuilt and the fire rekindled only when the people return in the new exodus prophesied by Isaiah. Theology, knowledge about God, has to be recast out of the new experience we have to have of God in the exile where God's people are waiting for liberation. The people's liberation has to do with God, and not just with our organizations. The Bible is one of the means which enables the people to be in permanent contact with God.

Where Do We Start the Work of Evangelization?

I spent six days in a little village of sixty-eight houses. We left there very early one Saturday morning, around half past four. Gradually the sky lightened and the sun rose over Macambira. They had been six very difficult days. Mounted on my donkey, I rode along thinking. I kept looking back, not along the road, but in my mind. I thought about the six days of my life I had left there, and about the people who had stayed behind. My thoughts included many questions and doubts which I am going to try and express here.

There were then six families living there, on the border between the states of Ceará and Piauí, in a sandy region which is neither mountain nor scrubland, hot, dry, and flat, ringed by mountains and scoured by the wind. From above it looks like a dried-up lake. Social ties had linked the various families so tightly that people said, "We're all just one family here." It was a natural system of organization which helped these people not to fall into total despair, and to keep their heads high, in spite of everything.

It was a community in which self-awareness was still a closed bud; they depended for the present on the stimulus their own activities gave them. It was a life of dependence: on the past and on tradition, which moved life forward in very slow steps. It was a life very tied to traditions as it was tied to the land; the past still gave life its shape. New things which found their way in were a shock, since they appeared like a force threatening to break everything apart. The people were conservative by nature. It was a community where history seemed to have stopped or, better, a community which world history had forgotten to take with it on its journey toward the future. And in that state it was being integrated into the new world system, a system the people did not know..

In the current situation the past no longer has sufficient power to carry this community forward. The new world is growing around it and penetrating into every cranny through the radio, new roads, cars, salesmen, markets, advertising, through the young man who went south, through the young man who returned from the south, through the new priest with different ideas, through the boss who lives out of the area but controls its inner workings. The vehicle of tradition and the past are falling apart and running out of gas.

The old patriarchs of the six dominant families have either already died or are becoming feeble, and are totally unable to assess the new world which is springing up around them, on the other side of the mountains. As a result, the new world gets in without scrutiny, since the internal resistance of the past and tradition have already been broken, and instead of being a "conservative" force (in the good sense of the term) and an integrating force, this combination of past and tradition is in grave danger of becoming reactionary. I heard an old man saying to his children, who were listening respectfully, "Children, you can't complain. I've never heard of a quarter-kilo of flour fetching 140 cruzeiros as it does today."

If it is true that the liberating word of the gospel has to be grafted on to the creative word, then we must ask this question: Is the life shaped by the creative word for these people in their situation today capable of receiving and supporting the Good News of the liberating word? As I thought about this question, I could find no answer.

The donkey I was riding said nothing. The sun rising over Macambira said nothing. Macambira said nothing. None of them said a word. They were unaware of the question forming in my mind. And yet something told me that nature, the sun, Macambira, and the animals have something to tell us through the way they live. It is all a question of profound respect for the laws of nature, the laws of growth, the cycles in the evolution of things, instinct which relies on billions of years of experience. The logic of a few days cannot make this untrue, just as a fish cannot destroy the water to which it owes its life. It would be its death.

I visited that village for six days. I saw mostly the external aspects of things, like glancing at a tree and seeing its external features and general shape. From glancing at a tree one can see the shape of the trunk, the arrangement of branches, the flowers and leaves, and one knows something of the systems within the tree supplying it with water and other nutrients. And yet one knows there are other complex systems which one cannot see by glancing at a tree, systems that give it life. Likewise, I could guess at the existence of invisible forces that held that village together, and I could guess about them based on my observations of the different types of relationship which existed in the community: between parents and children, between husband and wife, between godparents and godchildren, between godparents and parents, between landowner and tenant, between the families. There were relationships of production, relationships with traders, buyers, and sellers, at market and in the shops, relationships with the teacher, with the mayor, with the distant and unfamiliar government of the country. There was a system for making flour, planting the fields, spinning cotton, raising cattle. There was a nutritional system, a health and sanitation system, a system for the children's education. And there were relationships with God, with religion, with the saints, with the sacred, with the priest from the neighboring parish, with the bishop who came there from time to time—relationships for transmitting life-values. All these were what I could observe of the complex systems which make up the village "tree." Where on this tree must the gospel be grafted so that it can produce its fruit?

At this point that other question came back: What is the gospel for? And an earlier question also reasserted itself: Is the faith community only an instrument for changing society? It is one thing to give a theoretical reply to this last question, but another to find a practical answer for specific action in that village. Ideas came and went, running through my head; "the world ran past on the hooves of my donkey," and the miles slipped away behind me. The reply did not come. I am no longer worried about my ignorance.

CONCLUSION: CHRISTMAS NIGHT—GOD IS THE LIBERATOR!

It was a strange night. The gospel spoke of the birth of Jesus: "Joy for all the people: today your liberator has been born" (see Lk. 2:10–11); "his name is Emmanuel, that is, God-with-us" (Mt. 1:23). From the altar I could see an enormous mass of people, unknown faces looking at me. Poor people, rural people. Humble, hardworking people. All looking at "Father," who was giving them this "lovely present" of Christmas Mass. People looked at me, the priest, as though at a messenger from God. I could see they wanted to depend on me as they depend on God for their faith, their hope, and their love. But this only humbled me, for there at the altar it was clear to me that the priest depends on those people as he depends on God for his faith, his hope, and his love. It was clear to me that the people and priest depend on each other.

That night all my ideas seemed ridiculous. God had become incarnate in the lives of these people. God had not become incarnate in my ideas and theories about the people. God had become incarnate in this life, which multiplied and reproduced itself without the help of my ideas and theories.

I think that I, on that cold, windy night, dreary and frustrating, might have understood something of the great mystery of God the liberator who enfolds us in the midst of the people. What a strange thing! My ideas and explanations are not able to contain it! The plans which emerge from these ideas are unable to express the totality of the freedom God offers; they are insufficient to express the totality of the life whose seed God has placed in us. Something is missing. What is missing?

Maybe what is missing is the angels singing "Glory to God in the highest heaven, and on earth peace for those he favors" (Lk. 2:14). Maybe what is missing is an ability to live the gratuitousness of God's love for us. A keen experience of this gratuitousness can give plans consistency. It can fill life and give it a new meaning. A plan I devise, however certain and correct it may

be, leaves me uncertain and insecure. I do not have the courage
to offer it as a blueprint for the lives of others.

God-with-us! God is already with us. "While you were still
sinners, he died for you." We do not deserve it. Both life and
the liberation that comes from God—these and all else are
grace. Pelagius denied the gratuitousness of God, as did the
Pharisees. The ordinary people, by nature and through their
situation in life, live gratuitousness. How many times have I
heard people say, "Live! If it wasn't for God I couldn't survive.
No one looks after us. Those who hold power and wealth only
think of themselves!" And how many times have I heard this
other remark, so revealing of the attitudes of the poor, "Love,
yes, I love them. In spite of everything I love them. I love them
in God. If it wasn't for him, I don't know if I'd love them."
Because of the pressure for efficiency in the present system, and
because of the oppression and injustice of that system, which
destroys so many people's lives, the temptation today is not to
give sufficient attention to the gratuitousness of the gospel and
to look at it almost exclusively as an instrument for preserving
the status quo or changing an unjust world. But the change will
be genuine, radical, and really revolutionary, subversive of all
immoral systems which do not respect life, only when it arises
from the experience of God's gratuitous love for us.

I was at the end of my "postgraduate course"—that is, six
months in the hinterlands. The six months had left me with a
sense of deep weakness and ignorance. We are nothing. God is
the one who calls and saves, and that is why we have the courage
to do something. Those months had succeeded in creating in me
a sense of the need to spend time being useless before God, in
spite of all the work and the needs I thought were important.
They had succeeded in creating in me a greater concern with
the small details of human relationships, and with "wasting
time" on these details so that the suffering of the struggle may
be lightened a little. They had succeeded in creating in me a
firmer conviction that the gospel is first and foremost of the poor
and for the poor, and that we all have to learn from them. They
had enabled me to see the unimportance of many things which
had formerly seemed essential, and had thereby made me a little
freer within myself. One can have much more life with many

fewer things. They had enabled me to see the need for celebration if the struggle is to succeed. They had made me see more clearly the need for a deeper study of society, to identify more precisely the mechanisms which destroy life. They had made me understand that the gospel requires us to take up the cause of the poor, the innumerable poor, and to start looking at the world's problems from their point of view. Those six months had done a lot. I do not know if all this will triumph in me. Please God it will.

4

Biblical Theology in Brazil Today

INTRODUCTION

I am in a place without a library and have no chance to consult books. My only resources are my memory of the things I have learned and lived, the presence of my fellow religious, the backdrop of the communities, the poverty of the region and the cry of the people, which God hears and which I will not seek to stifle. As a result, this essay will not be complete. It will merely serve to initiate a debate, a debate in which, I hope, it will be corrected and amplified.

I shall try to reply to a question I was asked: "How is biblical theology done in Brazil today?" I shall offer my answer under three headings: (1) developments to date, (2) important issues, and (3) the main difficulties. I might have included a section called "the relationship between reflection and pastoral practice," but there was no need to do that, because everything I say will be the product of the interaction between reflection and pastoral practice.

I cannot define what "biblical theology" might be. There is no agreement on the matter. I understand the term to mean the effort to bring to light, with the help of the Bible, God's signs and calls in our lives and in external events.

I shall speak from my experience, what I see and do. It is a limited perspective, but I have no other. I shall not speak as a spectator watching the game from the stands and not participating. I shall be speaking from the position of someone playing on a team and wanting to win, but obeying the rules of the game and accepting the referee's decisions.

DEVELOPMENTS TO DATE

Pope Pius XII's encyclical *Divino Afflante Spiritu* set off in Europe a renewal of exegesis and an enormous interest in the Bible on the part of ordinary people. The renewed study of the Bible fed into theology, stimulated the liturgical renewal, and was the main force in the internal renewal of the church.

The exegetes who started the biblical movement here in Brazil were trained in Europe. They brought here the new wind which was blowing over there. Brazilian exegesis was an extension of European exegesis. The great majority of the works published in Brazil were translations of European authors or inspired by them. Nevertheless there was a very determined effort in Brazil to popularize the results of academic research in exegesis, which bore abundant fruit, and is still doing so today.

Exegesis in Brazil did not strike out in new directions. It did not open up new fields of research. It followed the principles of the method adopted by European exegesis, which, in general were (and still are) literary and historical. Very reliable principles, certainly.

For many years this biblical reflection was kept going and coordinated by the Liga dos Estudos Bíblicos (League of Biblical Studies—LEB). The LEB runs the *Revista de Cultura Bíblica (Review of Biblical Culture-RCB)* and even produced a translation of the Bible from the original texts. The translation was widely distributed in the edition known as "The Most Beautiful Bible in the World."

This whole renewal of study and reading of the Bible bore fruit at Vatican Council II, and was expressed in the synthesis of the document *Dei Verbum,* the tranquil product of a long struggle.

These days a certain weariness can be felt in European exegesis. The resources of the method adopted have been exhausted. There has been a constantly increasing specialization, which, however, does not seem to meet the demands of people living out their faith in the crises of a changing society. Academic exegesis has moved away from the lives of the people and no longer knows what its specific role is in the overall task of living the faith. There is a search for new directions, which are now beginning to be glimpsed here and there.

Academic exegesis no longer has the courage it had in the first half of this century, when, with excellent results, it criticized the overly dogmatic use of the Bible in the church. Today it no longer has the same courage to see and criticize the overly dogmatic use of the Bible, both inside and outside the church.

This crisis is reflected here in Brazil. The LEB is no longer able to channel the efforts of exegetes, who tend to go in different directions. The *Revista de Cultura Bíblica* barely survives. Few people buy the more specialized academic works. The people have different needs.

But there is something very new! Here in Brazil a new "biblical theology" is emerging. This new development does not come from the exegetes trained in the official schools. It comes from a different quarter. It comes from the ground, where the seed of the word of God was cast. It comes from the people, who have taken back the Bible and have started to read the word of God starting from the problems of their lives and struggle.

This popular reading of the Bible is the great new phenomenon which the Spirit is raising up among us and which has never existed in quite the same form before. It is the product of a series of convergences:

1. some exegetes' previous and continuing work of popularization;
2. the renewed liturgical movement, which has created greater interest in the Bible;
3. the Catholic Action movement, which helped to link the Bible with ordinary life by its "see, judge, and act" method;
4. biblical weeks promoted in many dioceses and parishes;
5. courses run by a number of organizations in various areas of Brazil;
6. the distribution of millions of Bibles;

7. the challenge of the sects, which use the Bible more than Catholics;

8. the abandonment of the poor, both by the government and by the church: these abandoned people discovered an ally in the word of God;

9. the influence of the Medellín and Puebla documents, which advocate a critical interpretation of society and attempt to re-read the documents of Vatican II on the basis and in the context of the Latin American situation;

10. the political situation of repression, which forced work with the people's organizations to be lower-key and more discreet;

11. the wind of change, which encourages skepticism and suspicion of things imposed by authority;

12. the action of the Holy Spirit, breathing strongly among the poor.

This new "biblical theology" which is germinating in the basic ecclesial communities finds expression in the way the people read the Bible. For the moment it is only a spoken theology, at once weak and strong, like the spoken word in general. It is not written down. It is transmitted in a different way than written scholarship, not through published books, but through an oral tradition, through celebrations and blessings, stories and plays, poems and songs, meetings, courses, visits, parties, and assemblies. This is exactly what happened with the word of God itself, before it received its written form in the Bible.

The vision and attitude which characterized the interpretation of the Church Fathers are reappearing in a new and surprising way when the people of the communities read the Bible. Despite all its defects and failings, this reading of the Bible by the poor creates a new context which enables academic exegesis to rediscover its mission in the church. In other words, it offers exegetes a new framework within which it is possible to rediscover what the "ministry of the word" needs to be in the church, even the ministry of those whose life is taken up in academic study of the Bible. And it will show the immense importance of academic study of the Bible.

How the Poor Read the Bible

The following are some of the features which characterize the reading of the Bible by the poor in the base communities.

COMMUNITY READING

The Bible is seen as the community's book. Even if they read on their own, the people know they are reading "the book of the community." The *sensus ecclesiae* reappears here in a new way. In the people's meetings, where the human word can circulate freely among the members of the community, the word of God produces freedom and there comes into being a *sensus ecclesiae,* a common meaning which the community discovers and adopts. In many places the use of the Bible has been de-clericalized. The people have reclaimed it as "our book," "written for us," as St. Paul said.

HISTORY AND MIRROR

The Bible is read not just as the history of the past but also and primarily as a mirror of the history taking place now in the lives of the people. Here we see again, in a new form, the vision of the Church Fathers, who talked of "letter" and "Spirit." There is a stress on the relevance of the word of God. God speaks to us today through life, illuminated by the Bible. The main purpose of reading the Bible is not to interpret the Bible, but to interpret life with the help of the Bible. The axis of interpretation has shifted because the concept of revelation is different.

SEARCHING FOR THE MEANING-FOR-US

The people's main concern is not the search for the (historico-literal) meaning-in-itself, but for the meaning the Bible has for us today. We find here, in a new form, all the questions raised by the idea of the "spiritual meaning": the meaning which the Spirit reveals to its church today through the ancient texts of the Bible.

A Prayerful Reading

In academic exegesis (perhaps not in theory, but in practice), faith is not the constitutive element of the process of interpretation. It is a prior condition. For the people, reading the Bible is faith itself in action. When they meet to read the word of God, they surround the reading with prayer. Always. Theirs is a prayerful reading. Here we find, in a new form, the *lectio divina*. The discovery of the meaning is not the product of scholarship alone, of human reasoning, but is also a gift of God through the Spirit. Room is given for the action of the Holy Spirit in the reading and interpretation of the Bible.

A Militant Reading

The people take the word of God seriously. They do not read simply in order to understand; they try also to put the word into practice. This is where conflict arises. This is where we meet the problem of the bearing of the word of God on the particular situation of today, which is political, social, and economic. We were taught the purpose of reading is to gain *information.* The way the people read is directed to *action,* to changing the situation. By that very fact reading takes on a political dimension. We can say the same thing in biblical terms: the way the people read the Bible reveals, very practically, the inherent role of the Bible to "announce" and "denounce," and leads to conversion.

A Reading from a Different Social Position

The people read the Bible from their situation of oppression within today's society. This enables them to discover a meaning which the exegetes did not discover because they were in a different social position. The people do not read neutrally. Their reading is engaged, committed to the poor and the struggle of the poor. Academic readings seek to be "objective," but there is no such thing as an "objective reading," if by that term one means a neutral reading. There can be an "objective reading" of the Bible only if one uses the term to refer to a reading set on clarifying the objective (purpose, goal) of the Bible and on making a practical contribution to the attainment of that "objective." Here, also, it should be remembered that the words "oppressor" and "oppressed" do not come from Marxist analysis, nor from left-wing ideology or any particular social theory. They are words which are part of the core of the Bible itself. Any Hebrew dictionary will confirm this. In using these terms the people are faithful to the word of God.

AN ALL-EMBRACING READING

What this means is the following. Searching for and discovering a meaning do not take place solely or primarily through discussion, classes, information, and reasoning, but through a much broader process which involves all aspects of life: human contact, celebrations, the shared struggle, meetings, community organizing. The people's concept of "the word of God" and "the gospel" is much broader than just the written word. It is much closer to the Bible's concept of "the word of God" and "the gospel."

A New Vision: A Sign of the Kingdom

The way the people read the Bible, which I have attempted to describe above, is intermingled with the confused situation in which the people of the communities live their faith. As I said before, there are many defects and inadequacies in the people's reading of the Bible. But the root is sound. It is the purest tradition. The vision with which the people read the Bible and the attitude they take to interpreting it are much more in the center of the tradition than the vision and the attitude to interpretation adopted by modern academic exegesis. Modern exegesis has a new vision which makes the Bible an old book. The people have a new vision which makes the Bible a new book.

The way the people read the Bible is a gift from God to the church, a gift which will require the most careful attention and also obedience on the part of those who have been appointed to serve the people and to watch over the purity of the faith. Through the gift which God is raising up today among the people God is saying something to all of us. The way the people read the Bible is a tiny seed which promises abundant fruit, if the plant is allowed to grow, if it is well nurtured and watered by the gardeners, and pruned if necessary.

This is the extent of the information I have to give about the process so far. Not everything is clear. There are many questions and doubts, but the tree is known by its fruits. One sign of the coming of the kingdom is when the blind begin to see, the lepers are cleansed, the dead rise, and the poor are evangelized. These signs, given by Jesus himself, are already becoming reality. The blind see, cripples walk, lepers are cleansed, the dead are rising, and the poor are not merely being evangelized but are themselves evangelizing.

IMPORTANT ISSUES

This new situation regarding the people's reading of the Bible appeals to all of us not to "stifle the voice of the Holy Spirit" and to have the courage "to be guided by the Spirit," as St. Paul told the Christians of the communities in Thessalonica and Galatia. In view of this a number of important issues require special attention. They are more theoretical issues concerned with the process of interpretation and the content of the biblical message.

Issues Involving the Process of Interpreting the Bible

THE PURPOSE OF INTERPRETATION

What is the purpose of interpretation, the discovery of the meaning-in-itself or of the meaning-for-us? The problem is very ancient, going back to Origen. In his address to the Italian exegetes, which I have cited in previous chapters, Pope Paul VI touched on this issue when he said that: "Interpretation will not have completed its task until it has shown how the meaning of scripture can be related to the present moment of salvation, that is, when it demonstrates its application in the current situation of the church and the world. . . ." The limited role of exegesis in the narrow sense is one thing, and the wider task of hermeneutics is another. Exegesis has invaded the process of hermeneutics and taken it over. Paul VI, in his address, was trying to put matters right. It is necessary to define more accurately the role of exegesis in the strict sense in relation to the broader aims of hermeneutics.

THE INTERPRETER

Is the interpreter the individual, the exegete closeted with his or her scholarship, or the community? What exactly is the *sensus ecclesiae*? Those who insist most firmly that they are defending the authority of the pope in the interpretation of the Bible run the risk of eliminating the role of the community, the church. They restrict the authority of the magisterium to the few texts whose meaning has been defined by the pope and explain other texts with complete freedom. This leads us to ask a number of important questions about biblical interpretation: How are we to integrate the action of the Holy Spirit present in the community, the authority of the magisterium, and the essential role of scholarship? How can we harmonize these elements into one and the same process of interpretation? What in practice is the role of the faith community in the interpretation of the Bible? How can this community help the exegete in his or her scholarly research?

PRINCIPLES FOR INTERPRETATION

Pope Pius XII, in his encyclical *Divino Afflante Spiritu,* insists on two types of principles, those of faith and those of scholarship. The principle most used by the people of the communities is the situation of life today. Can life today as it is lived in Latin America be a principle of biblical interpretation? Pope Paul VI, in his address to Italian exegetes, talked of the need to look for a "connaturality" of interests and problems between the situation of the peoples of the Bible and the situation of people today, if we are to be able to hear and discover the meaning God has placed in the Bible for us. In what way can a new social situation in Latin America, which did not exist in the time of the Bible, contribute to the discovery of the meaning of ancient texts?

THE SOCIAL POSITION OF THE INTERPRETER

From what social position should a Christian interpreter read and interpret the Bible? What is the right social position? What was the social position from which the Bible was produced? Jesus said: "I bless you, Father, . . . for hiding these things from the learned and the clever and revealing them to these little ones. Yes, Father, for that is what it pleased you to do" (Mt. 11:25–26).

INTERPRETATION AND THE OPTION FOR THE POOR

Today there is an effort to interpret the Bible from the position of the poor and for the poor. But, in itself, the process of interpretation does not yet belong to the poor. It is something done by educated people. The poor have difficulty getting access to it. For the moment the option for the poor is present in the motivation and the results of biblical interpretation. It has not yet penetrated to the heart and structure of the process of interpretation as such. Can that be achieved? Is it necessary? What would interpretation be like if we took seriously the option for the poor and allowed it to become a constitutive element of the process of interpretation itself?

THE METHOD OF INTERPRETATION

We were trained in the method of literary and historical criticism in its various forms. These days new methods are appearing, capable of revealing unsuspected riches within the biblical texts. Some exegetes use the method of sociological analysis. Others prefer the method of linguistic or structural analysis. Others continue to use the methods in which they were trained. Others use different methods again. Which method best equips us to discover what God has to say to us today through the text of the Bible? What are the strengths and weaknesses of each method? Which of them is most useful in responding to the demands the people of the communities make on the "ministers of the word"? What are the reasons for the reservations expressed by Pope John Paul II about the so-called "re-reading of the gospels"?

PATRISTIC EXEGESIS

What exactly is the vision with which the people of the communities read and interpret the Bible? In what way is the vision which the Church Fathers had of the Bible being taken up anew by the people of the communities? It would seem to be of crucial importance to examine patristic exegesis more deeply to enable us to demonstrate the "legitimacy" of the interpretation of the

Bible being produced by the people of the communities. This would also help to eliminate possible prejudices against the people's interpretation on the part of priests and bishops.

Scholarly Interpretation and the People's Interpretation

How can the one assist and benefit the other? In general the two types of interpretation coexist without much contact or dialogue. They ignore each other, and this is bad for both. Scholarly exegesis rejects the "pious" interpretations of the people and treats them as examples of *sensus accomodatus*. The people, for their part, do not pay any attention to scholarly exegesis because very often they cannot understand a word of what exegetes say. What contribution could the people's interpretation make to a better employment of scholarly exegesis? What could scholarly exegesis do to give more substance to the people's interpretation of the Bible?

Issues Involving the Content of the Biblical Message

Liberation

The people of the communities interpret the Bible within a perspective of liberation. This is not just another theme alongside all the other biblical themes. It is a new way of looking at things which arises out of the Bible itself. The liberationist dimension of Christian faith, the analysis of society in terms of oppressors and oppressed, and the exploration of the bearing of the message on economic, social, political, and religious structures are not the product of some modern ideology, but are dictated by fidelity to the word of God itself.

Revelation

The people of the communities understand revelation as God speaking today through what happens in the world. Revelation belongs to the present. "God's message is part and parcel of life." The attitude of many priests to revelation is that it belongs exclusively to the past. It has been established in the deposit of faith, to be preserved, defended, passed on, and taught to the people by the guardians of the faith, the pastors. It follows that the pastors do not need to listen to the people. Their mission is to pass on and teach. It is therefore possible that, in the future, pastors, in the name of received revelation, may become the grave-diggers of the "gift of God" which the Holy Spirit is offering the church through the poor.

CREATION AND SALVATION

What is the relationship between creation and salvation? According to St. Augustine, the Bible was given to us not to replace the "book of life" (creation), but to help us to "decipher the world," to restore to us "the eye of contemplation"; thus the purpose of interpreting the Bible is "to transform the world into a great theophany" or revelation of God. Accordingly, the political dimension is inherent in the very word of God. It is an element of tradition, not some arbitrary modern invention. Those who insist on trying to separate faith and politics, evangelization and social change, are arguing on the basis of a quite recent tradition, and seem to ignore the great tradition which goes right back to the Fathers of the Church.

GRATUITOUSNESS AND GRACE

In a world in which everything is done and organized on the principle of efficiency, what sense can we make of the gratuitousness of God's action? The question applies both to those who, in the name of faith, are opposed to change and to those of us who, in the name of faith, are struggling for the transformation of society. Action for change requires planning and efficiency, and yet, at the same time, it remains true that only God is the liberator. The people of the communities, despite all their struggles, are able to live and celebrate the gratuitousness of the gift of life and the victories in the struggle. They continue to seek strength for their journey in mysticism. Many, however, the more they become involved in the struggle, feel that the church has little to offer to give them strength. This is because we have been insufficiently radical in making mysticism and prayer relevant. Mysticism has a liberational and political dimension, as past history shows. We need a new spirituality.

FATHER, SON, AND HOLY SPIRIT

In the Bible the battles against the false gods of the totalitarian systems of the period led the prophets to fight savagely to defend the true image of God, whom they called Yahweh. What false image of God is propagated today by totalitarian systems which call themselves Christian? How much are these false images in the eyes of us, the interpreters, when we explain the Bible to the people? What image of God does the Bible transmit to us? What image of Jesus is most in harmony with the Bible itself and with the demands of the journey being undertaken by the people of the communities? What exactly is the action of the Spirit in the church and the world? The light which may come from the discussion of these central questions may illuminate the answers to many of our other questions.

FAITH IN THE RESURRECTION

What does faith in the resurrection mean for us today? Is it simply belief in the immortality of the soul, or faith that the people, inspired and strengthened by Jesus and his Spirit, are able to face and overcome the forces of death (active in life) with the same power that the Father used to rescue Jesus from death? The resurrection does not fit into scientific models; there is no room for it. How can it influence scientific analysis of society and how can it inspire, in quite practical ways, the people's struggle to win their rights as children of God?

MINISTRIES

The question of ministries is rarely studied in relation to the Old Testament, in which the various "services" were part of God's overall plan for God's people. Some New Testament texts which speak of ministries are not given due weight in the present practice of the church. For example: "Whatever you bind on earth will be bound in heaven." This "order" is given by Jesus to three different levels of persons: to Peter (Mt. 16:19), to the apostles (Jn. 20:23), and to the community (Mt. 18:18). In present practice this "order" of Jesus is reserved for Peter and the apostles. No one thinks of conferring such power on the community itself. Why?

These are some of the important themes which require deeper reflection. This deeper reflection could do much to reduce the internal conflicts or tensions in the church. Knowledge of the Bible and tradition is often blocked by prejudices which are not always based on the Bible and tradition.

THE MAIN DIFFICULTIES

There are many problems and difficulties which threaten to strangle this new life emerging amid the people. We saw some of them when I listed the important themes. Here I want to list a few more which come to mind.

The Prevailing Wind

Some sections of the hierarchy have reservations about the basic ecclesial communities. There is a real danger that the whole new movement which is growing up may be co-opted by an institution which sees the communities as the threat of a sort of parallel church. The fear is not based on reality. There is a great lack of dialogue.

The Training of Priests

The phenomenon of the basic communities cannot be neatly and completely categorized within the structures of the training given in seminaries. Because of this many priests feel incapable of giving the people the support they keep pleading for. They are unable to see the people's journey and struggle in the light of the word of God in such a way as to help the people to see what God is asking of them within their life in society. This creates a distance between priests and the people of the communities, which is good neither for the priests nor for the communities.

The Bible of the Poor

In the past Christians were creative. For example, they invented the so-called Bible of the poor, reproducing the stories of the Bible in paintings on the walls of the churches. Today we must find ways to help the poor to discover means to continue this tradition of inventing a Bible of the poor. But this is no easy task, for the Bible is a book and yet the people of the communities, who are so attached to the word of God, very often can barely read, or cannot read at all. How can we ensure that access to the word of God is not made to depend on access to human scholarship, which makes knowing how to read and write a condition for understanding the word of God? How can we ensure that the faith of the "simple and the little children" does not become dependent on the knowledge of the "learned and clever"?

The Training of Biblical Scholars

At present, more than half the world's Catholics live in Latin America. It is predicted that around the year 2000 this proportion will have risen to three-quarters. In practice, however, those who lead the "service of the word" are being trained outside Latin America and are being taught to deal with issues which are not ours. To enable the new movement in the church to continue and spread its fruits throughout the church it is urgent that practical steps be taken to train biblical scholars here in Brazil and in the rest of Latin America, and it is essential that these scholars be taught to cope with the real problems of our people. Ensuring the continued "service of the word" is one of the chief obligations of pastors.

The Problems Raised by Ecumenism

There is an ecumenism which operates at an institutional level, and its practitioners try to analyze the differences and the similarities in the way faith in Jesus Christ is professed and celebrated. In the communities there is growing up, very timidly, an ecumenism in which Christians of different denominations unite—in the name of their common faith in Christ—to defend life and rights which are being crushed underfoot. It is in this way, practically, that they are overcoming their differences. But when those working at the institutional level try to instruct those in the communities about ecumenism and its doctrinal and theoretical complexities, then the process meets many difficulties and much resistance, from all sides. The practice of the people has much to teach us about how to overcome these difficulties and resistance. We must overcome them, for ecumenism is the touchstone of everything, above all in the use, reading, and interpretation of the Bible.

Epilogue: Two Prayers

PRAYER OF A PILGRIM

Lord God, I have gone through life looking for you. I asked your name and your address. I want to know the place where you live. I want to meet you and talk with you. But they gave me so many names and addresses for you that I ended up lost. My God, where do you live?

Some pointed me to great temples and churches. They said, "His name is Highest God!" I went there, but I didn't find you. I only found beautiful stones and complacent people who said they knew all about you. I wasn't able to believe in them, much as I wanted to. My heart told me, "God isn't like that." They only wanted to teach me things and put their ideas in my head, as if I knew nothing about anything. Among them I did not find justice or love.

Others pointed me to rebel groups living in the shadows. They said, "His name is the God Who Avenges and Punishes." I went there, but I wasn't sure. I met good people, but I didn't meet humility. They too only wanted to teach things and put their ideas in my head, as if I knew nothing about anything. Among them I didn't find the freedom they talk about so much.

I carried on, looking for your house, your presence. Tired and sweaty after walking so much, I stopped at the house of a poor man. He was sitting on the steps in front of his shack, enjoying the evening breeze. I asked him your address and your name. He said to me, "My friend, excuse my ignorance. My name is Severino. I can't give you any information, but come in and rest a little—you look worn out. However long you stay with me, this house is yours." I went in, and I'm still there, my God.

I don't know if you live in Severino's house. He tells me he doesn't know you. But in his company I have found peace and humility, sharing and forgiveness, solidarity and struggle for justice. I have found complete freedom. Answer my question, God: Are you hiding in this poor man's house?

You must be! He doesn't come on like a teacher, and he's taught me so much. He has nothing, and he's given me all I needed. He calls himself ignorant, but he knows much more than I. He is weak and without strength, but to this day no one has been able to defeat him in his struggle for justice. His life is full of suffering, but I've never found so much happiness. He lives in struggle, but radiates peace.

If this isn't where you live, Lord, I don't know where else to look. Here I find and receive what I sought, and here I will gladly stay until you show me a better home. I only hope that one day you will reveal your name to me. Amen!

PRAYER FOR THE REBORN WORLD

A child is born. The world has begun again (Psalm 151).

> Lord, you are our hope,
> the rock that supports our lives.
> Your word is always before us.
> It does not abandon us, by day or by night.
> Your promise is peace and sharing,
> justice and forgiveness your trademark!
>
> In your people's heart you have placed a spring
> which can turn into a rushing river,
> tributaries in each of our hearts
> to water the soil of our land,
> to water the seeds and quench the thirst of our children.
>
> We are rubbish. We beat our breasts. Forgive us.
> On guard at the entrance to our consciousness,
> we left the door open and the robbers got in.
> They stole the riches you gave us
> and now they are getting rich from our work.

They force us to give up all we have
and don't pay us the wage we have earned.

For a moment we even thought,
"They've won. God is on their side!
Let's do like them. They'll save us."
But it was our blindness which made us think like that.
They saw it and tightened the screw still more:
capped the spring, diverted the river,
dammed up the tributaries and hid the water.
They deprived your people of your presence and said,
"God is ours. He's given up on you.
The world is ours. God says so."

Like the hinterlands in a drought, our life is a desert.
Nothing but despair and loss rising in our hearts.
From the depths of our distress we call out to you, Lord.
As in the old days, hear our shouts.
And you did, Lord, you heard your people's shout for
    help.
Faithful to your promise, you came to save your people.
You upset the great and made much of the little ones.
The eyes of your people opened wide and they saw your
    wonders.

The dry ground sprouted green.
Happiness gushed from the cross.
Strength grew out of weakness
and life burst out of death.
Freedom returned from captivity
and wisdom sprouted among ignorance.
Riches appeared in the poor man's hands
and the virgin bore a son.

Lord our God,
the seeds of your kingdom are unfolding everywhere
and showing the presence of the spring that was hidden.
Among your people the spring grew,
the tributaries merged, and a garden appeared.

The river of your justice runs through our land again,
making the start of the future spring up on all sides.

Your peace can now be seen by all.
Your justice has taken shape as sharing,
and your people have begun to celebrate the certain
    victory.
The news of your presence breaks in throughout the
    land.
The sun confirms it and tells the stars.
The moon swears to it and beams it through the night.
The rivers transmit it to the endless sea,
and the vapor it gives off carries the news to the clouds.
The whole world is already celebrating your good news
which fills the lives of the little ones with hope:
"A child is born. The world has begun again!"

Lord, you are our hope,
the rock that supports our lives.